PHONICS PRACTICE BOOK

Teacher's Edition

Kindergarten

Harcourt

Orlando   Boston   Dallas   Chicago   San Diego

Visit The Learning Site!

www.harcourtschool.com

ISBN 0-15-325778-4

1 2 3 4 5 6 7 8 9 10   073   10 09 08 07 06 05 04 03 02 01

CONTENTS

Name_____

Mm

Have children name and trace the letter Mm at the top of the page. Ask them to find and mark the letter Mm in the mittens.

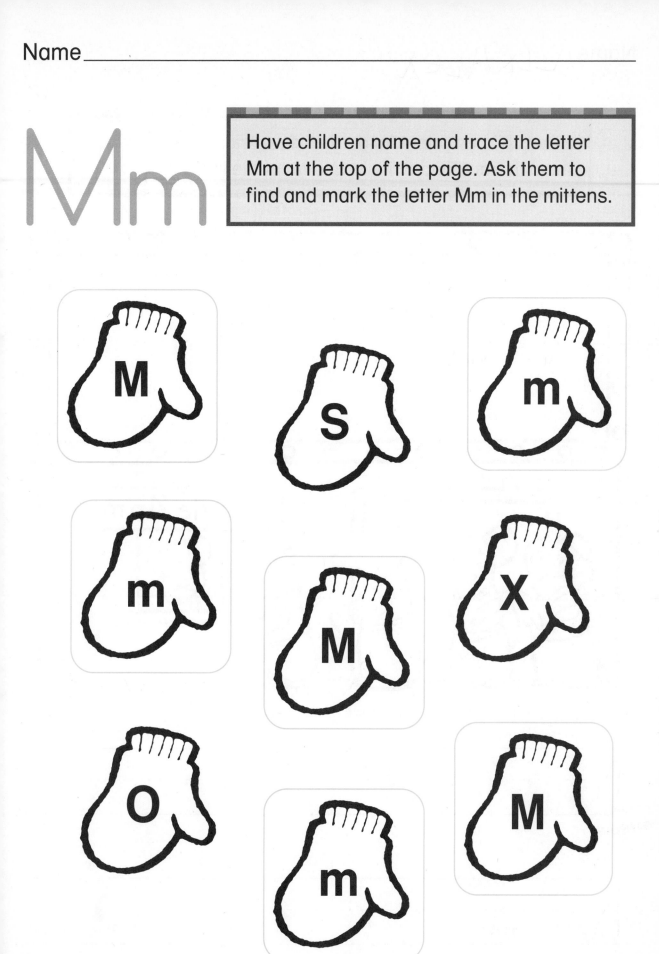

Name ALEx Alex

Have children print Mm on the movie sign. Then ask them to trace and write M and m on the lines.

Name _ALEX_

Have children name each picture and color the items whose names begin with the /m/ sound, as in *mouse*.

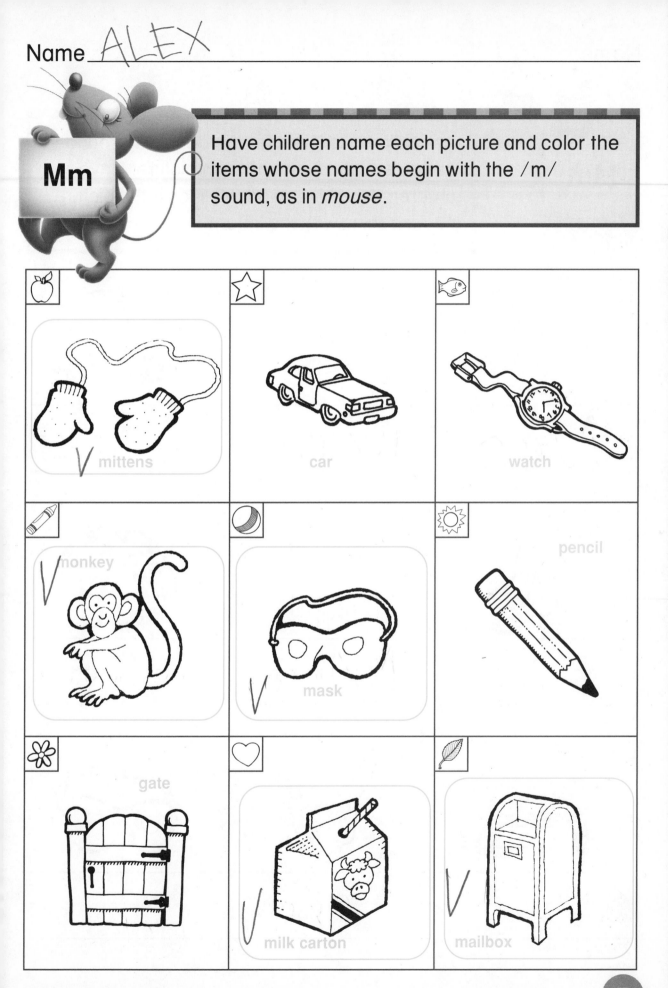

✓ mittens

car

watch

✓ monkey

✓ mask

pencil

gate

✓ milk carton

✓ mailbox

Name_____

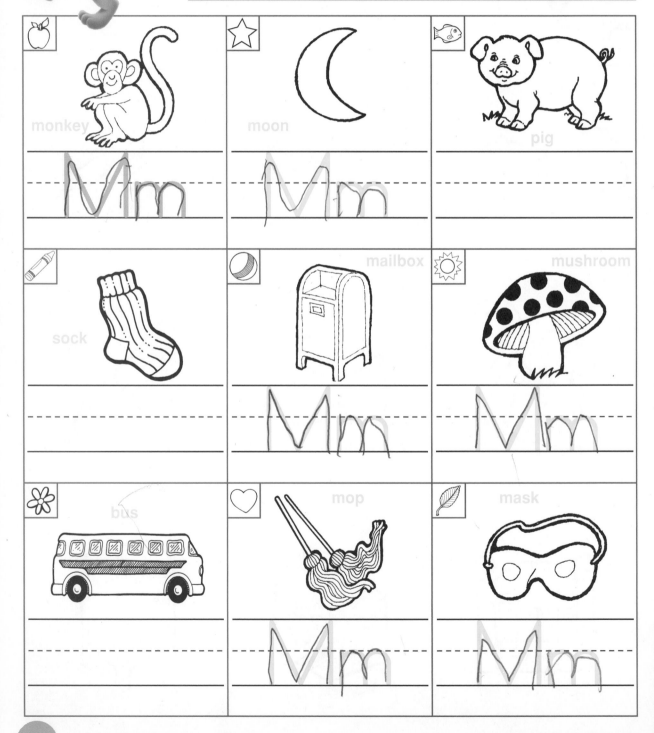

Mm

Ask children to listen for the beginning sound as you say the name of each picture. Have children write M or m on the lines if the picture name begins with the letter Mm.

monkey — Mm

moon — Mm

pig

sock

mailbox — Mm

mushroom — Mm

bus

mop — Mm

mask — Mm

Name_____

Ss

Have children name and trace the letter Ss at the top of the page. Ask them to find and mark the letter Ss in the socks.

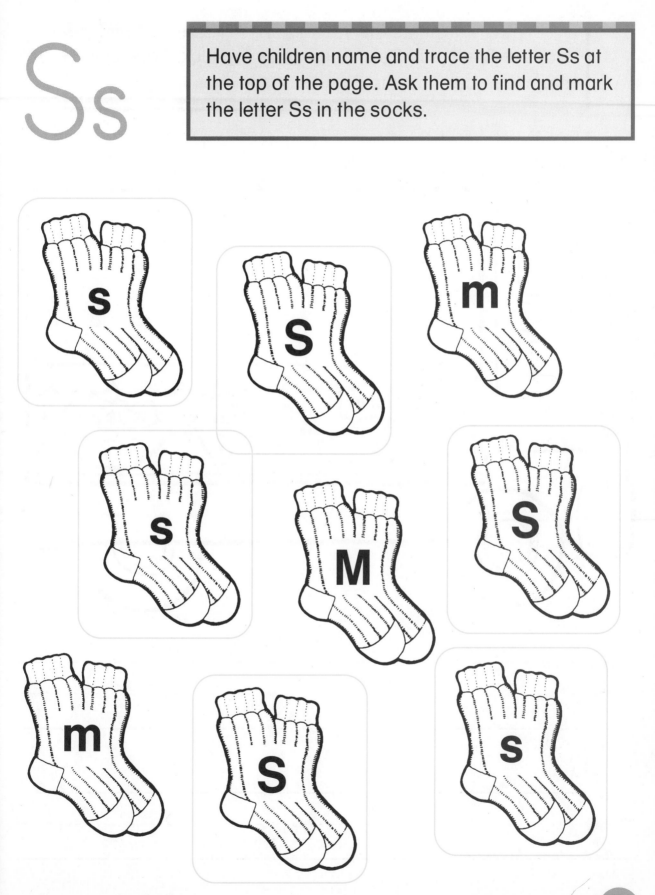

Name_____

Have children print Ss on the sandwich truck. Then ask them to trace and write S and s on the lines.

SSSS   ss ss

SSSS   ss ss

Name _____

Ss

Have children name each picture and color the items whose names begin with the /s/ sound, as in *seal*.

sandal	sink	bicycle
jet	horse	sun
socks	desk	sandwich

Ss

Ask children to listen for the beginning sound as you say the name of each picture. Have children write S or s on the lines if the picture name begins with the letter Ss.

saw

zebra

sandbox

_____
Ss

_____

_____
Ss

sock

six

sink

_____
Ss

_____
Ss

_____
Ss

nurse

sun

turtle

_____

_____
Ss

_____

Name_____

Rr

Have children name and trace the letter Rr at the top of the page. Ask them to find and mark the letter Rr in the rings.

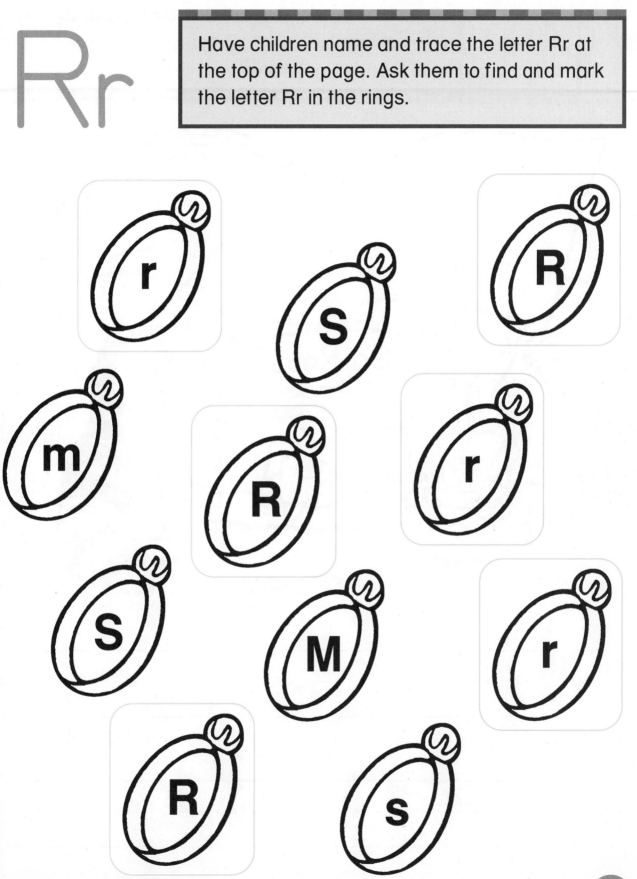

Name_____

Have children print Rr on the race flag. Then ask them to trace and write R and r on the lines.

R R R R   r r r r

R R R R   r r r r

Name_____

Have children name each picture and color the items whose names begin with the /r/ sound, as in *rabbit*.

rake

ladder

moon

rug

robot

raccoon

zebra

ring

sandal

Ask children to listen for the beginning sound as you say the name of each picture. Have children write R or r on the lines if the picture name begins with the letter Rr.

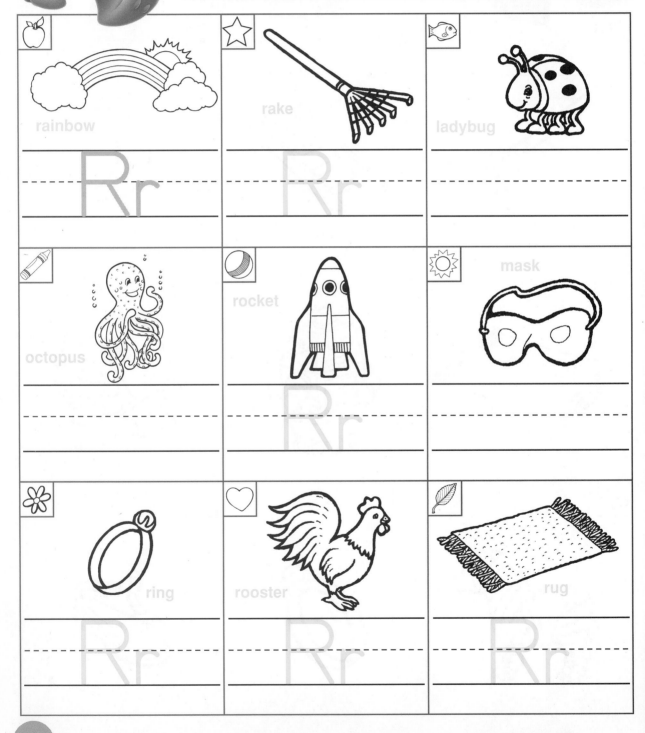

rainbow

rake

ladybug

octopus

rocket

mask

ring

rooster

rug

Name_____

Tt

Have children name and trace the letter Tt at the top of the page. Ask them to find and mark the letter Tt in the tops.

Name _____

Have children print Tt on the zoo sign. Then ask them to trace and write T and t on the lines.

Name_____

Tt

Have children name each picture and color the items whose names begin with the /t/ sound, as in *turtle*.

TV	ring	kite
pencil	tape	toothbrush
panda	top	towel

Name_____

table

turkey

wagon

sandwich

tiger

ten

cat

tomato

toothbrush

Name_____

REVIEW

Say the name of each picture. Then have children circle the letter that stands for its beginning sound.

monkey

r   **t**   **m**

rake

s   **m**   r

rose

r   **s**   **t**

towel

s   **t**   **m**

mask

m   r   **s**

seal

m   **s**   **r**

ten

s   **t**   r

sun

s   **t**   **m**

Name_____

Say the name of each picture. Then have children write the letter that stands for its beginning sound.

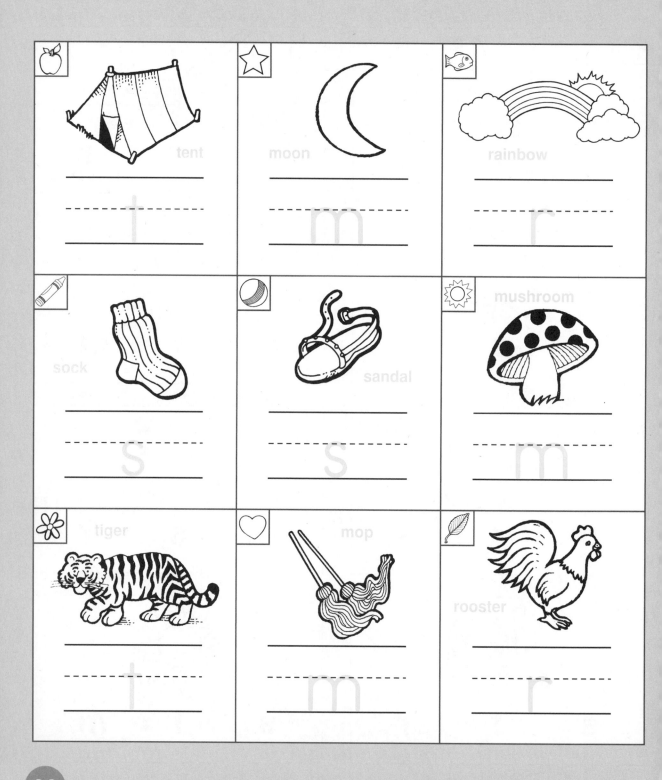

tent

moon

rainbow

_____

- - - - - - - - -

_____

sock

sandal

mushroom

_____

- - - - - - - - -

_____

tiger

mop

rooster

_____

- - - - - - - - -

_____

Phonics Practice Book

Name_____

Pp

Have children name and trace the letter Pp at the top of the page. Ask them to find and mark the letter Pp in the pumpkins.

 M

 S

 p

 P

 t

 P

 m

 P

 p

 P

T

Name_____

Have children print Pp on the pet store sign. Then ask them to trace and write P and p on the lines.

PPPP   ppp

PPPP   pppp

Name_____

Pp

Have children name each picture and color the items whose names begin with the /p/ sound, as in *penguin*.

puppet	mouse	cat
dog	pizza	popcorn
pencil	fish	piano

Name_____

Pp

Ask children to listen for the beginning sound as you say the name of each picture. Have children write P or p on the lines if the picture name begins with the letter Pp.

pig	pan	bus
pie	pencil	vest
pin	gate	pear

Phonics Practice Book

Name ALEX

Cc

Have children name and trace the letter Cc at the top of the page. Ask them to find and mark the letter Cc in the cups.

Name_____

Cat Castle

CCCC   cccc

CCCC   cccc

Cc

Have children name each picture and color the items whose names begin with the /k/ sound, as in *cat*.

moon

cup

car

corn

turtle

coat

panda

camel

sink

Name_____

Cc

Ask children to listen for the beginning sound as you say the name of each picture. Have children write C or c on the lines if the picture name begins with the letter Cc.

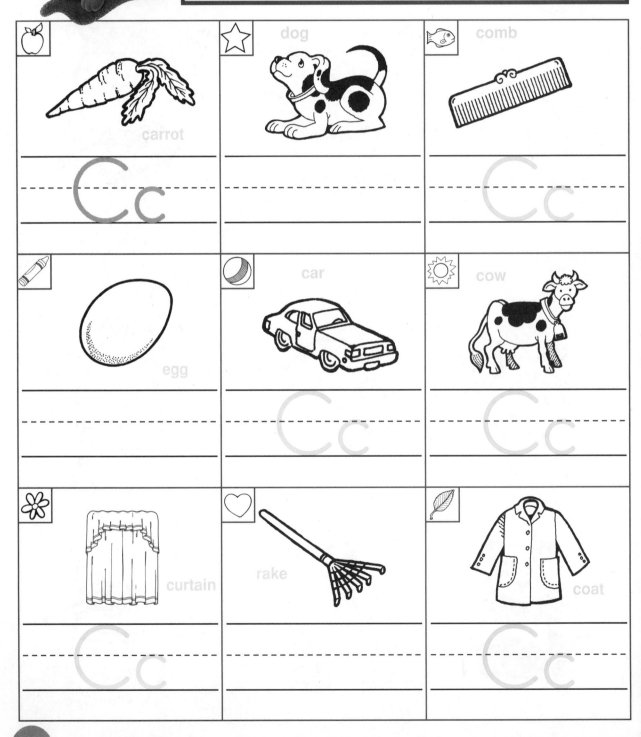

carrot

dog

comb

egg

car

cow

curtain

rake

coat

Name_____

Aa

Have children name and trace the letter Aa at the top of the page. Ask them to find and mark the letter Aa in the apples.

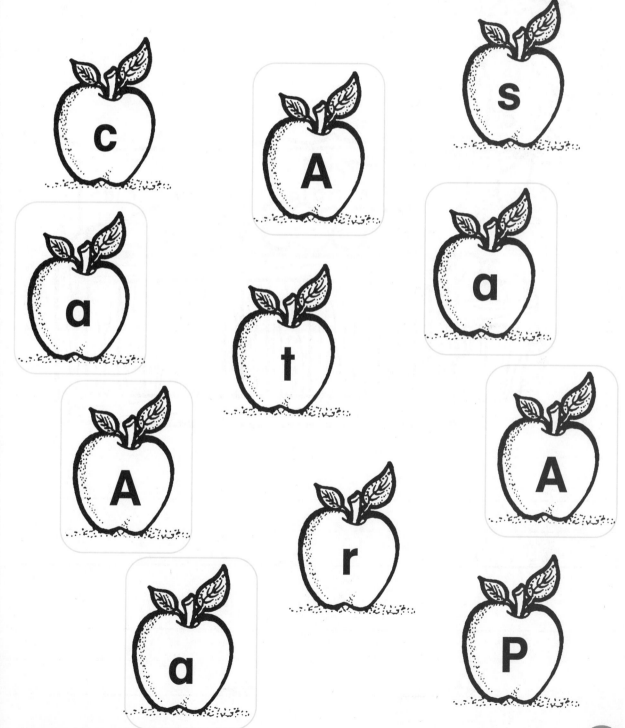

Name_____

Name_____

Aa

Have children name each picture and color the items whose names begin with the /a/ sound, as in *alligator*.

apple

anteater

zipper

leaf

axe

cup

ant

astronaut

door

Name _____

Aa

Ask children to listen for the beginning sound as you say the name of each picture. Have children write A or a on the lines if the picture name begins with the letter Aa.

astronaut	apple	axe
feather	ambulance	anteater
bear	ant	goat

REVIEW

Say the name of each picture. Then have children circle the letter that stands for its beginning sound.

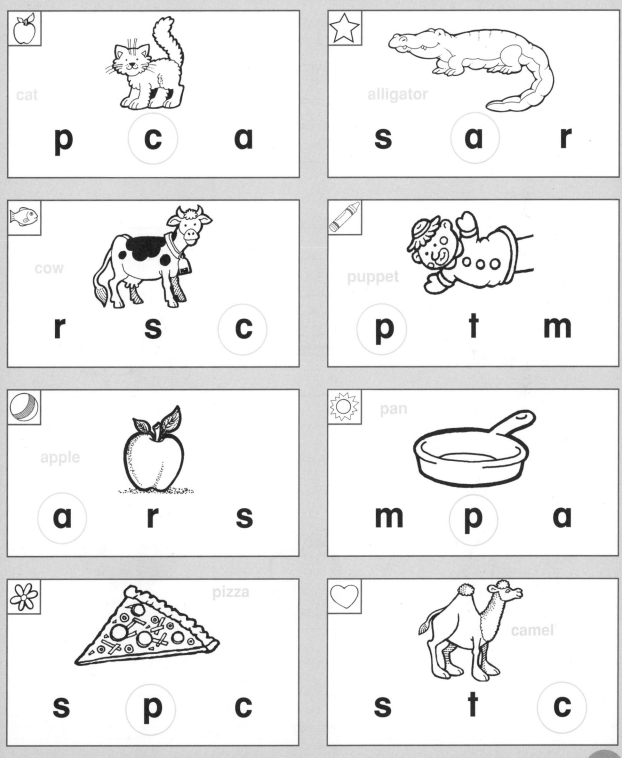

cat

p (c) a

alligator

s (a) r

cow

r s (c)

puppet

(p) t m

apple

(a) r s

pan

m (p) a

pizza

s (p) c

camel

s t (c)

Name _____

Say the name of each picture. Then have children write the letter that stands for its beginning sound.

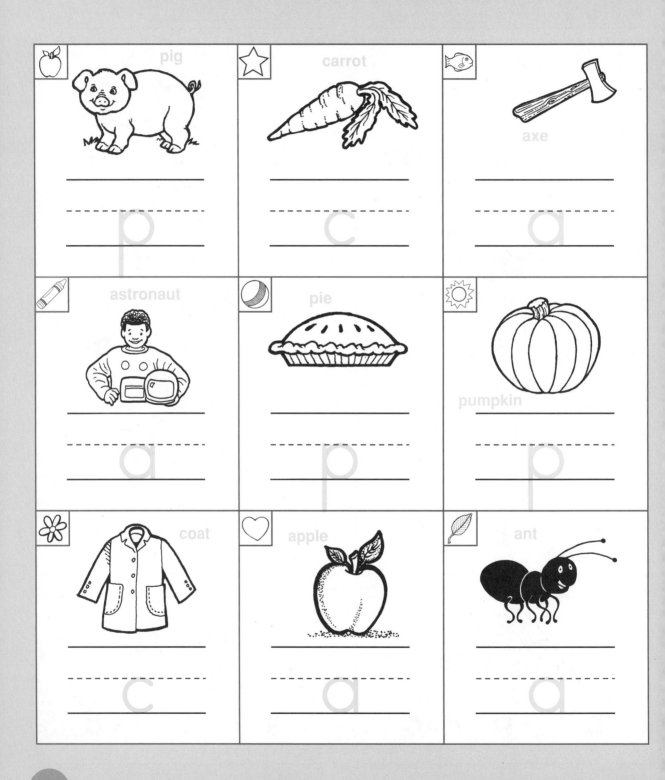

Name _____

Nn

Have children name and trace the letter Nn at the top of the page. Ask them to find and mark the letter Nn in the nests.

Have children print Nn at the top of the newspaper.
Then ask them to trace and write N and n on the lines.

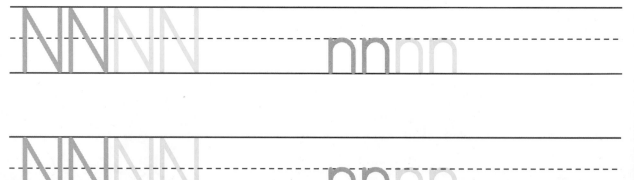

Name_____

Nn

Have children name each picture and color the items whose names begin with the /n/ sound, as in *newt*.

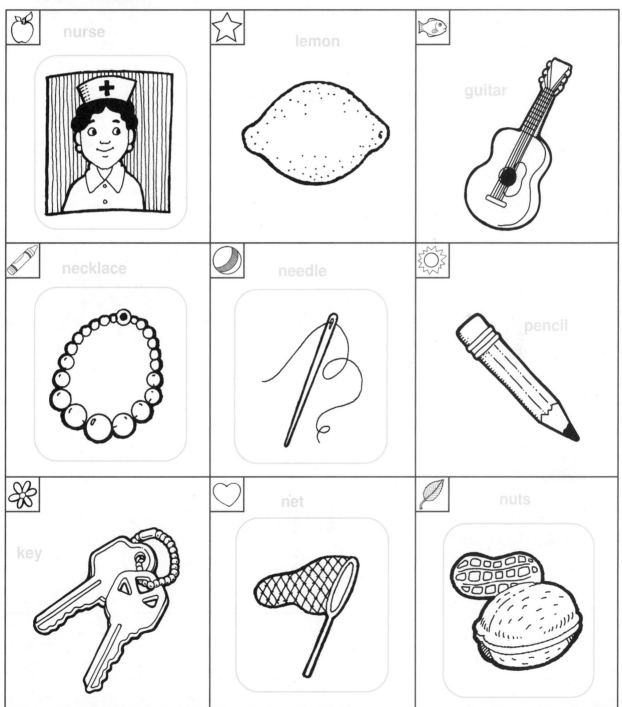

nurse	lemon	guitar
necklace	needle	pencil
key	net	nuts

Name_____

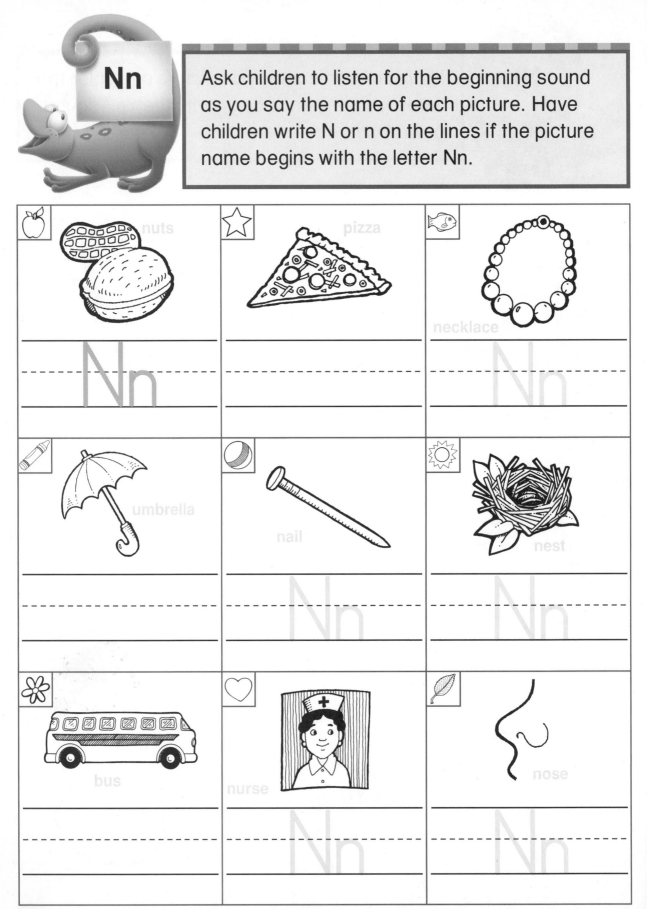

Nn

Ask children to listen for the beginning sound as you say the name of each picture. Have children write N or n on the lines if the picture name begins with the letter Nn.

nuts

pizza

necklace

Nn

Nn

umbrella

nail

nest

Nn

Nn

bus

nurse

nose

Nn

Nn

Name_____

Dd

Have children name and trace the letter Dd at the top of the page. Ask them to find and mark the letter Dd in the dinosaurs.

Consonant /d/d

Name_____

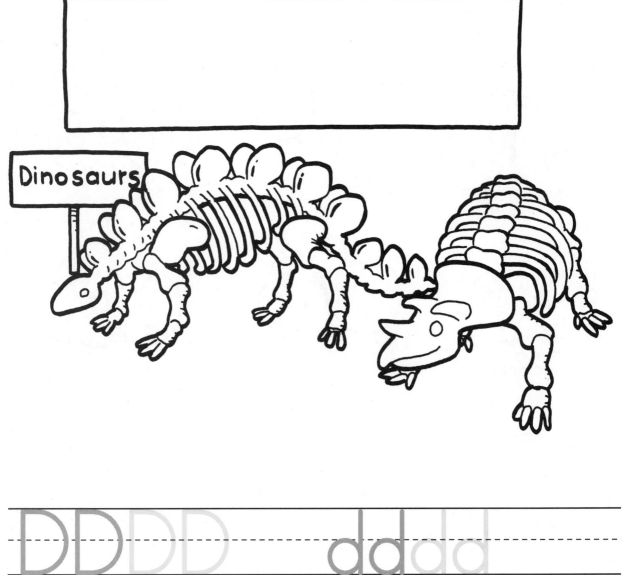

Dinosaurs

DDDD   dddd

DDDD   dddd

Name _____

Dd

Have children name each picture and color the items whose names begin with the /d/ sound, as in *duck*.

doll	apple	carrots
dog	horse	deer
desk	jet	doctor

Name_____

Dd

Ask children to listen for the beginning sound as you say the name of each picture. Have children write D or d on the lines if the picture name begins with the letter Dd.

dog

Dd

doctor

donkey

Dd

hat

doll

dinosaur

Dd

Dd

yarn

dish

door

Dd

Dd

Consonant /d/d

Phonics Practice Book

Name _____

Say the name of each picture. Then have children circle the letter that stands for its beginning sound.

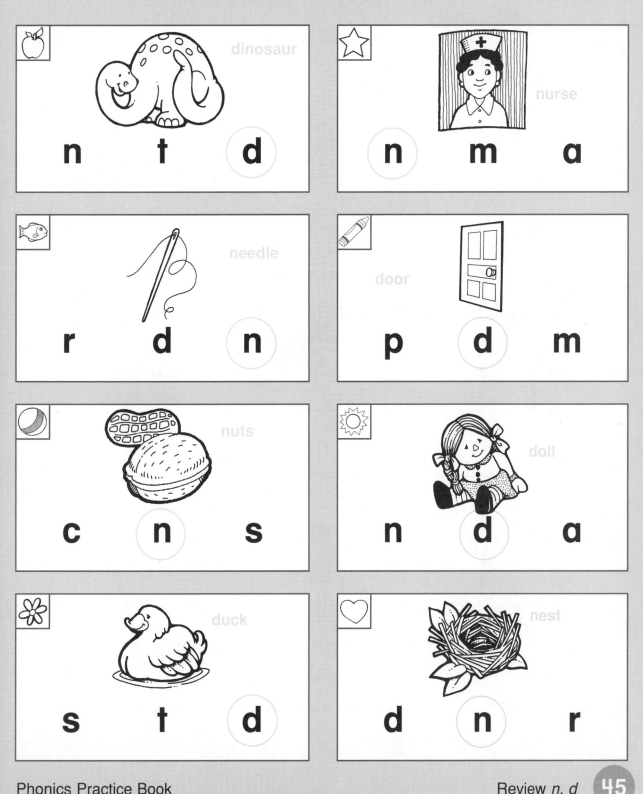

n   t   d

n   m   a

r   d   n

p   d   m

c   n   s

n   d   a

s   t   d

d   n   r

Say the name of each picture. Then have children write the letter that stands for its beginning sound.

net

n

nail

n

donkey

d

nurse

n

dog

d

desk

d

necklace

n

doctor

d

needle

n

Name _____

Gg

Have children name and trace the letter Gg at the top of the page. Ask them to find and mark the letter Gg in the gates.

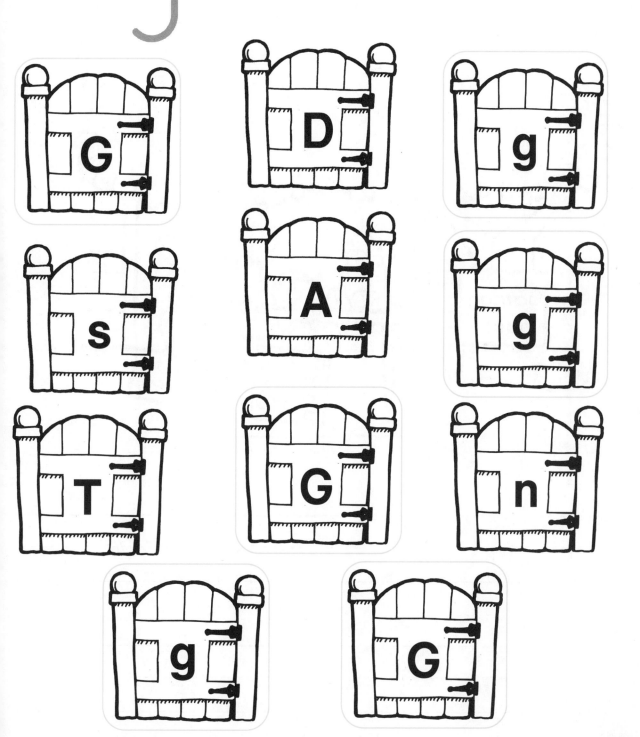

Have children print Gg above the garage sale. Then ask them to trace and write G and g on the lines.

Garage Sale

Guitar $50

GGGG gggg

GGGG gggg

Name _____

Gg

Have children name each picture and color the items whose names begin with the /g/ sound, as in *goose*.

gate

rooster

fork

goat

game

guitar

nest

girl

dinosaur

Name_____

Gg

Ask children to listen for the beginning sound as you say the name of each picture. Have children write G or g on the lines if the picture name begins with the letter Gg.

Name Alex

Ff

5/5 = A+
100%

d

f ✓

F ✓

F ✓

A

c

D

f ✓

F ✓

n

f ✓

Name_____

100%

Have children print Ff on the banner flying over the
farm. Then ask them to trace and write F and f on the
lines.

Fred

Fish
Pond

Fox
Farm

3

FFFFFFFF   ffffffff

3

3

FFFFFFFF   ffffffff

3

Name _____

Ff

Have children name each picture and color the items whose names begin with the /f/ sound, as in *fish*.

bear

girl

√ four

cow

√ fan

√ fox

tire

√ feather

√ football

Name_____

100%

Ff

Ask children to listen for the beginning sound as you say the name of each picture. Have children write F or f on the lines if the picture name begins with the letter Ff.

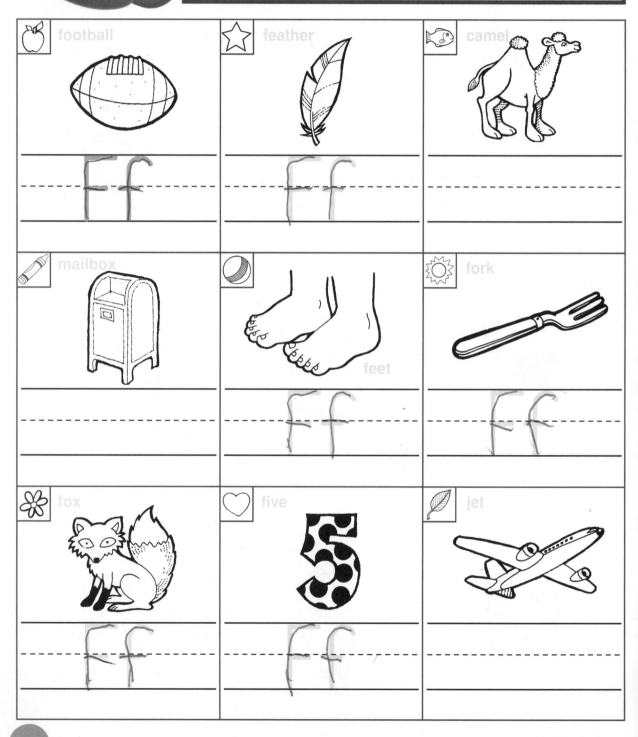

football

feather

camel

F f

F f

mailbox

feet

fork

F f

F f

fox

five

jet

F f

F f

Name _____

I i

Have children name and trace the letter Ii at the top of the page. Ask them to find and mark the letter Ii in the igloos.

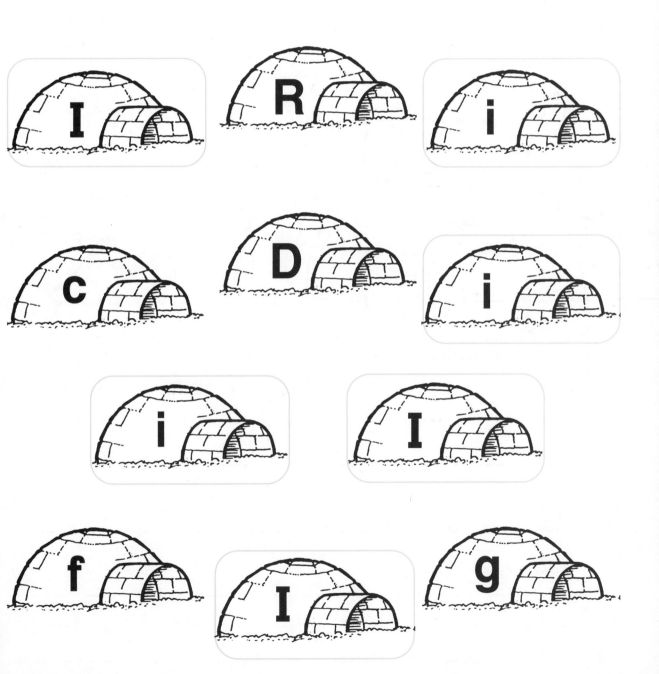

Name_____

Ii

Have children name each picture and color the items whose names begin with the /i/ sound, as in *iguana*.

igloo

valentine

cake

dog

inchworm

in

pineapple

fish

inch

Name_____

Ii

Ask children to listen for the beginning sound as you say the name of each picture. Have children write I or i on the lines if the picture name begins with the letter Ii.

Name **ALEX**

100%

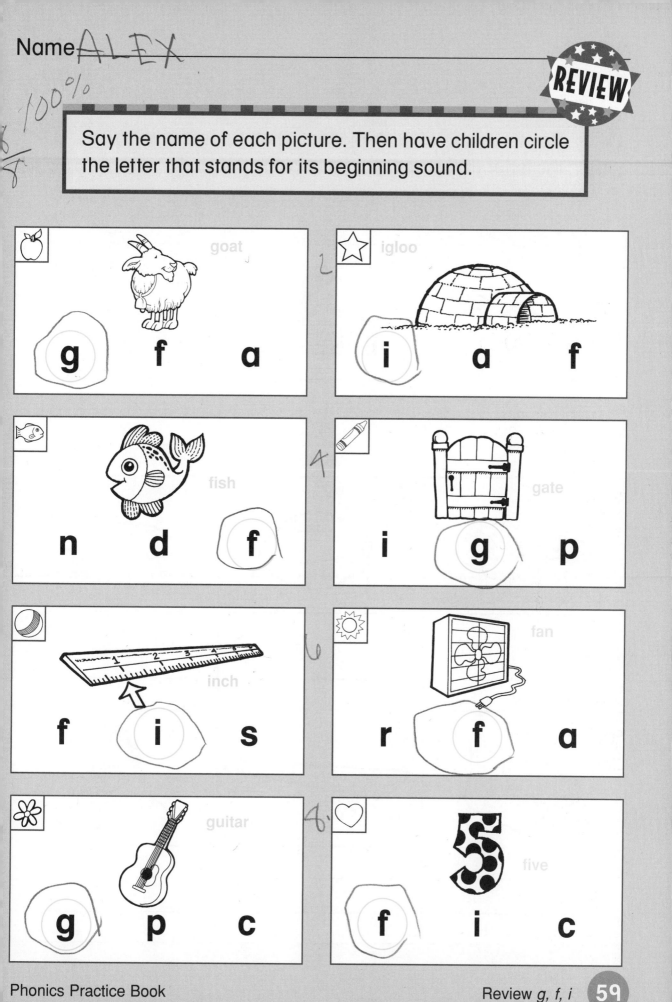

Say the name of each picture. Then have children circle the letter that stands for its beginning sound.

goat

g   f   a

igloo

i   a   f

fish

n   d   **f**

gate

i   **g**   p

inch

f   **i**   s

fan

r   **f**   a

guitar

g   p   c

five

f   i   c

Name_____

REVIEW

Say the name of each picture. Then have children write the letter that stands for its beginning sound.

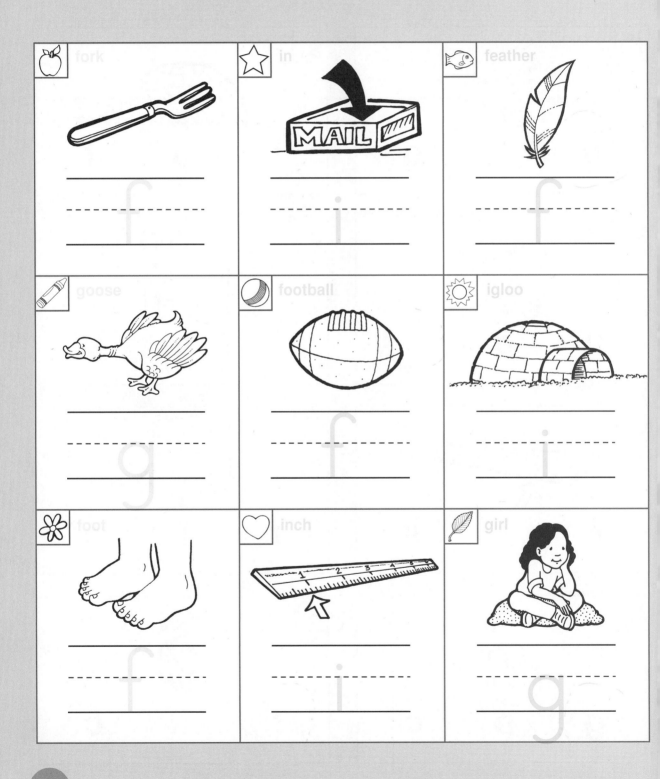

Review *g, f, i*

Phonics Practice Book

Ll

Name_____

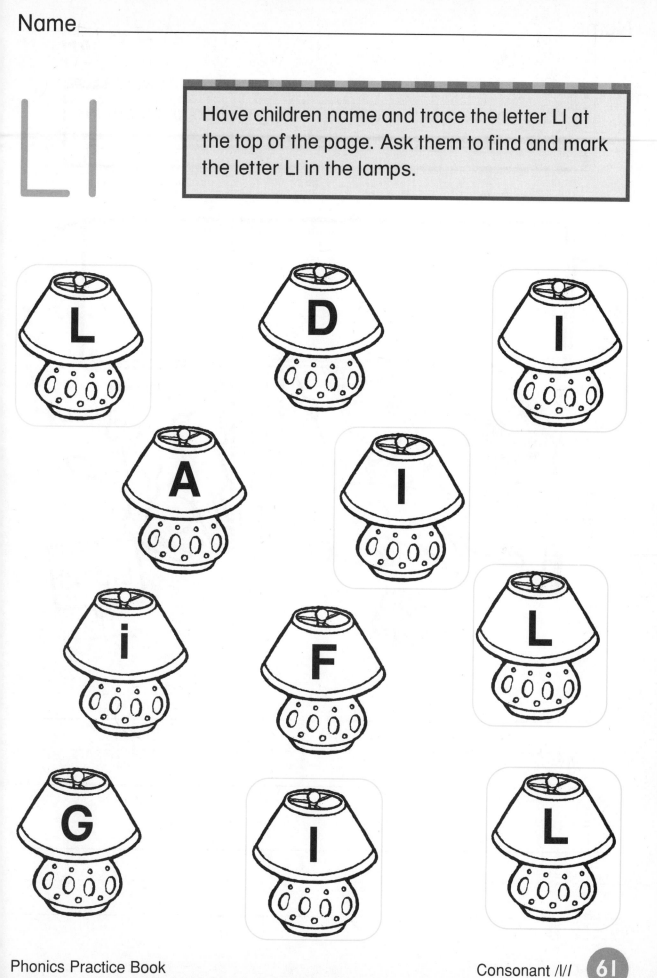

Have children print Ll on the zoo sign. Then ask them to trace and write L and l on the lines.

Name_____

Have children name each picture and color the items whose names begin with the /l/ sound, as in *lamb*.

mouse	leaf	lemon
ladder	feather	lion
igloo	ladybug	van

Ask children to listen for the beginning sound as you say the name of each picture. Have children write L or l on the lines if the picture name begins with the letter Ll.

ladder

mittens

lizard

rainbow

log

leaf

lettuce

bird

lamp

Name_____

Hh

Have children name and trace the letter Hh at the top of the page. Ask them to find and mark the letter Hh in the hearts.

Name_____

Have children print Hh on the roof of the house. Then ask them to trace and write H and h on the lines.

Consonant /h/h

Phonics Practice Book

Name_____

Hh

Have children name each picture and color the items whose names begin with the /h/ sound, as in *hippo*.

hat

horse

volcano

leaf

house

watermelon

hanger

heart

yarn

Name_____

Hh

Ask children to listen for the beginning sound as you say the name of each picture. Have children write H or h on the lines if the picture name begins with the letter Hh.

house

hand

king

hammer

elephant

hat

mouse

hot dog

helicopter

Phonics Practice Book

Name_____

Say the name of each picture. Then have children circle the letter that stands for its beginning sound.

ladder

l **h** **a**

horse

l **f** **h**

hot dog

n **h** **f**

heart

i **h** **p**

lion

h **i** **l**

lemon

r **l** **a**

helicopter

l **h** **c**

ladybug

f **l** **h**

Review *l, h*

Name _____

REVIEW

Say the name of each picture. Then have children write the letter that stands for its beginning sound.

hand

lamp

hanger

log

lizard

hammer

lettuce

hippo

house

Name_____

Bb

Have children name and trace the letter Bb at the top of the page. Ask them to find and mark the letter Bb in the beds.

B

R

b

c

H

b

b

B

f

B

g

Name_____

Have children print Bb on the side of the bus. Then ask them to trace and write B and b on the lines.

B Street Bus

BUS STOP

BBBB   bbbb

BBBB   bbbb

Name_____

Bb

Have children name each picture and color the items whose names begin with the /b/ sound, as in *bear*.

umbrella

mop

butterfly

ball

banana

house

lamb

book

bus

Name_____

Bb

Ask children to listen for the beginning sound as you say the name of each picture. Have children write B or b on the lines if the picture name begins with the letter Bb.

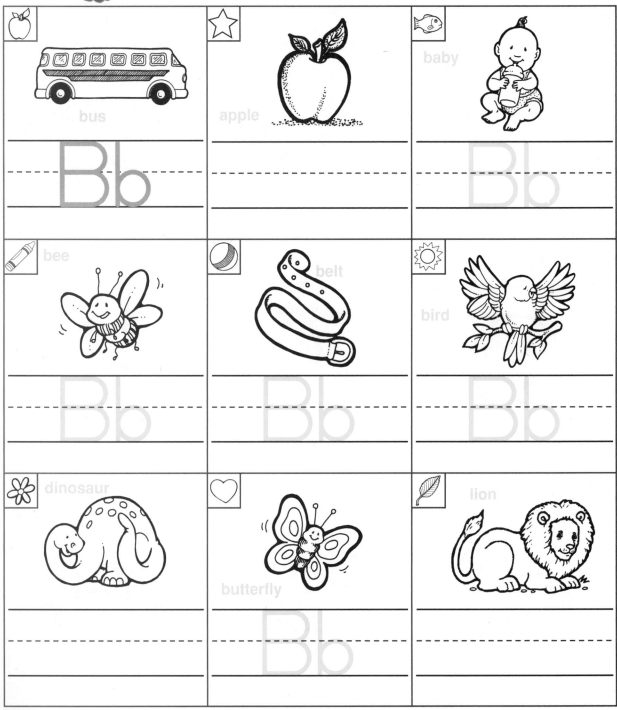

bus

apple

baby

bee

belt

bird

dinosaur

butterfly

lion

Phonics Practice Book

Name _____

Kk

Have children name and trace the letter Kk at the top of the page. Ask them to find and mark the letter Kk in the kites.

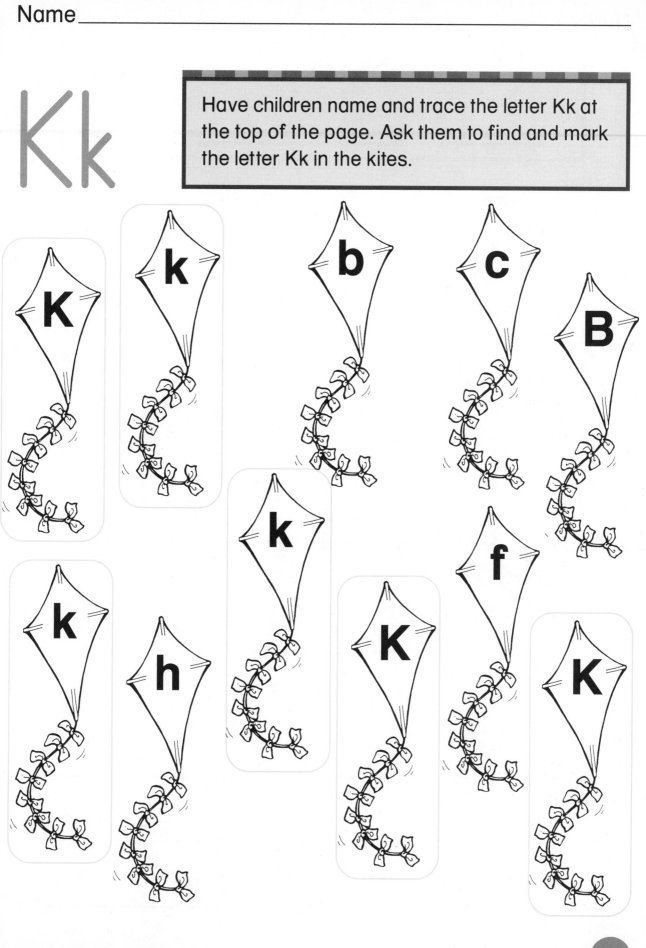

Name_____

Have children print Kk over the kitchen. Then ask them
to trace and write K and k on the lines.

K K K   k k k

K K K   k k k

Name _____

Kk

Have children name each picture and color the items whose names begin with the /k/ sound, as in *kangaroo*.

kite	keys	bicycle
elephant	needle	kitten
koala	pig	king

Name_____

Ask children to listen for the beginning sound as you say the name of each picture. Have children write K or k on the lines if the picture name begins with the letter Kk.

keys

hammer

king

fox

kitten

kite

kitchen

deer

koala

Name_____

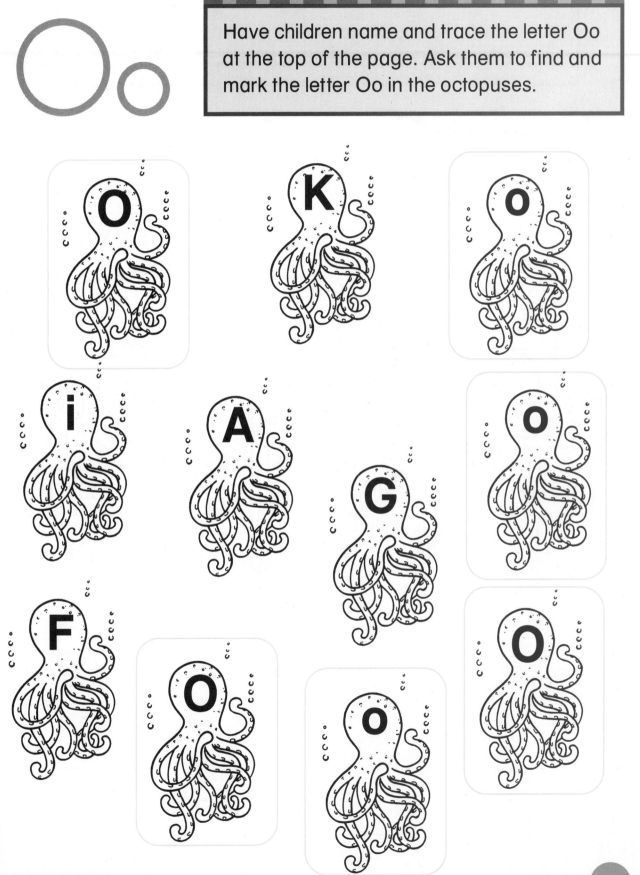

Have children name and trace the letter Oo at the top of the page. Ask them to find and mark the letter Oo in the octopuses.

O K O

i A G O

F O o O

Name _____

Have children print Oo on the flag. Then ask them to trace and write O and o on the lines.

Ollie
Ostrich

Oggie
Otter

Name_____

Oo

Have children name each picture and color the items whose names begin with the /o/ sound, as in *octopus*.

ostrich

tent

rake

olives

kangaroo

ox

hammer

otter

duck

Vowel /o/o

Name_____

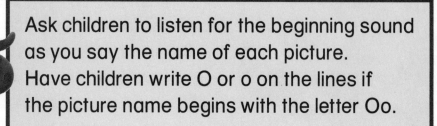

Oo

Ask children to listen for the beginning sound as you say the name of each picture. Have children write O or o on the lines if the picture name begins with the letter Oo.

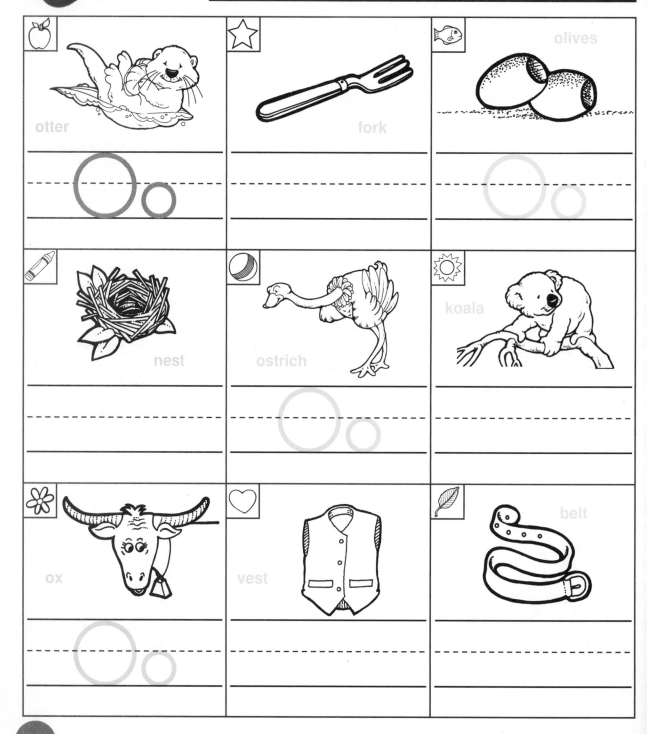

otter

fork

olives

nest

ostrich

koala

ox

vest

belt

Say the name of each picture. Then have children circle the letter that stands for its beginning sound.

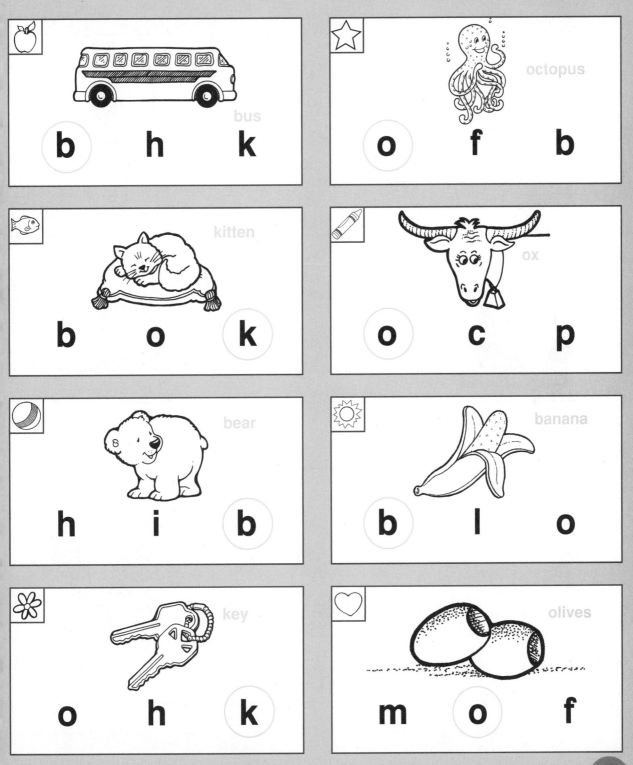

b   h   k

o   f   b

b   o   k

o   c   p

h   i   b

b   l   o

o   h   k

m   o   f

REVIEW

Say the name of each picture. Then have children write the letter that stands for its beginning sound.

kitchen

k

ostrich

o

ball

b

barn

b

kangaroo

k

olives

o

kite

k

baby

b

bird

b

Name_____

W w

Have children name and trace the letter Ww at the top of the page. Ask them to find and mark the letter Ww in the wagons.

Name_____

Have children print Ww on the laundromat sign. Then ask them to trace and write W and w on the lines.

Hot Water
Wash

WWWW   wwww

WWWW   wwww

Name_____

Ww

Have children name each picture and color the items whose names begin with the /w/ sound, as in *walrus*.

watch

jeep

kite

nest

window

web

alligator

wagon

wig

Name_____

Ww

Ask children to listen for the beginning sound as you say the name of each picture. Have children write W or w on the lines if the picture name begins with the letter Ww.

wagon	worm	alligator
W w	W w	
pumpkin	wig	water
	W w	W w
windmill	tire	watermelon
W w		W w

Name_____

Xx

Have children name and trace the letter Xx at the top of the page. Ask them to find and mark the letter Xx in the boxes.

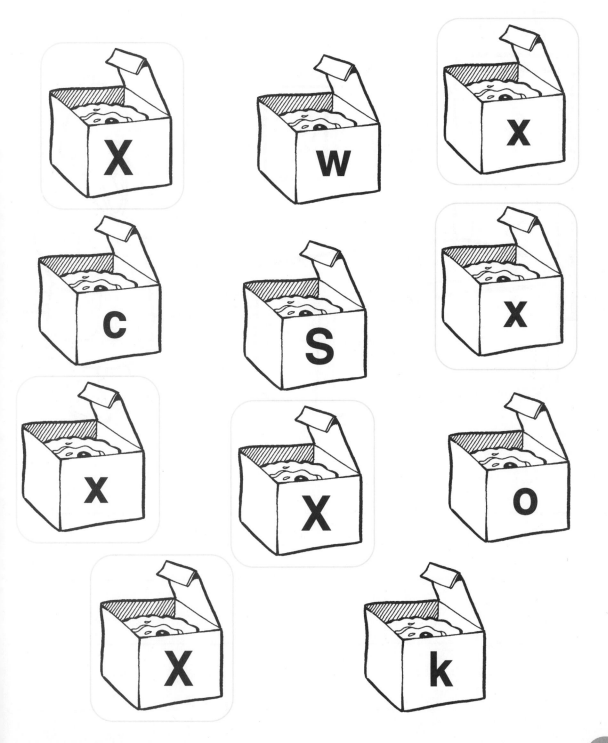

Name_____

Have children print Xx in the doctor's office. Then ask
them to trace and write X and x on the lines.

Name_____

Xx

Have children name each picture and color the items whose names begin or end with the /ks/ sound, as in *fox* and *x-ray*.

x-ray

monkey

cat

bee

box

axe

ox

umpire

six

Name

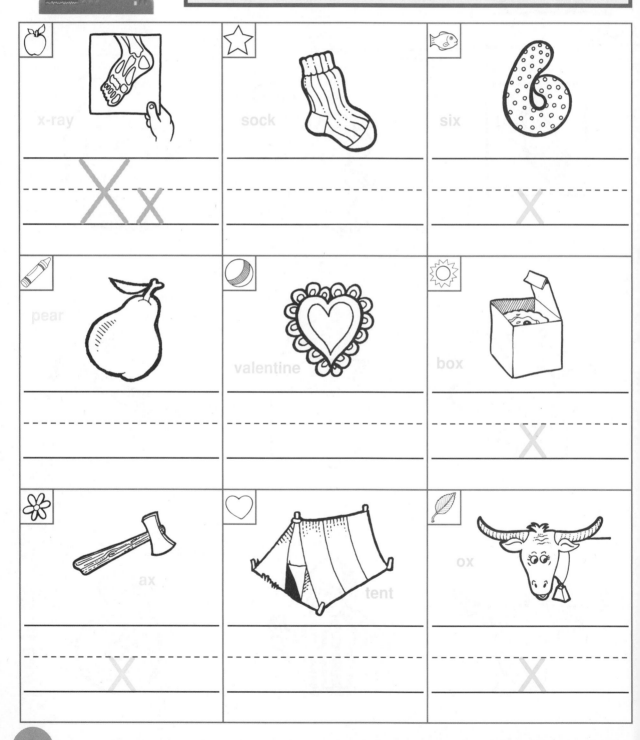

Xx

Ask children to listen for the beginning sound as you say the name of each picture. Have children write X or x on the lines if the picture name begins or ends with the letter Xx.

x-ray

sock

six

pear

valentine

box

ax

tent

ox

Name_____

Say the name of each picture. Then have children circle the letter that stands for its beginning or ending sound.

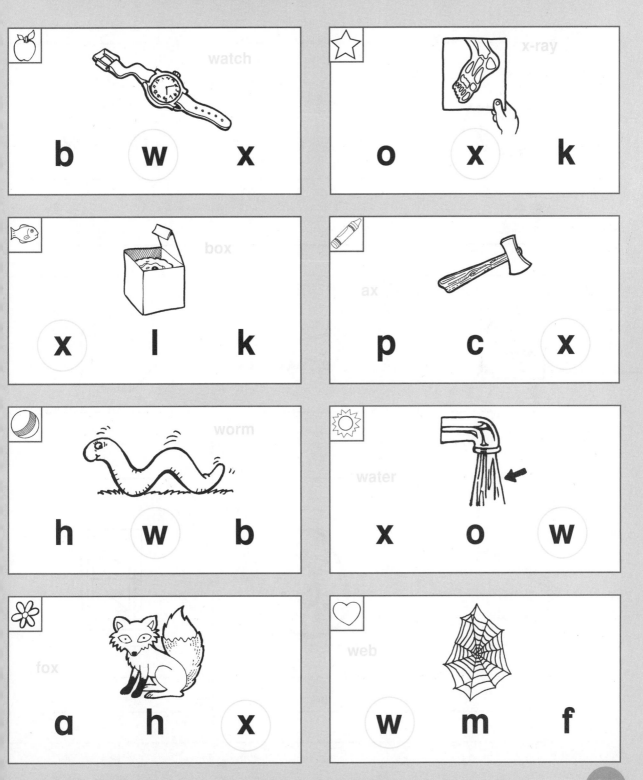

b w x

o x k

x l k

p c x

h w b

x o w

a h x

w m f

Name_____

Say the name of each picture. Then have children write the letter that stands for its beginning or ending sound.

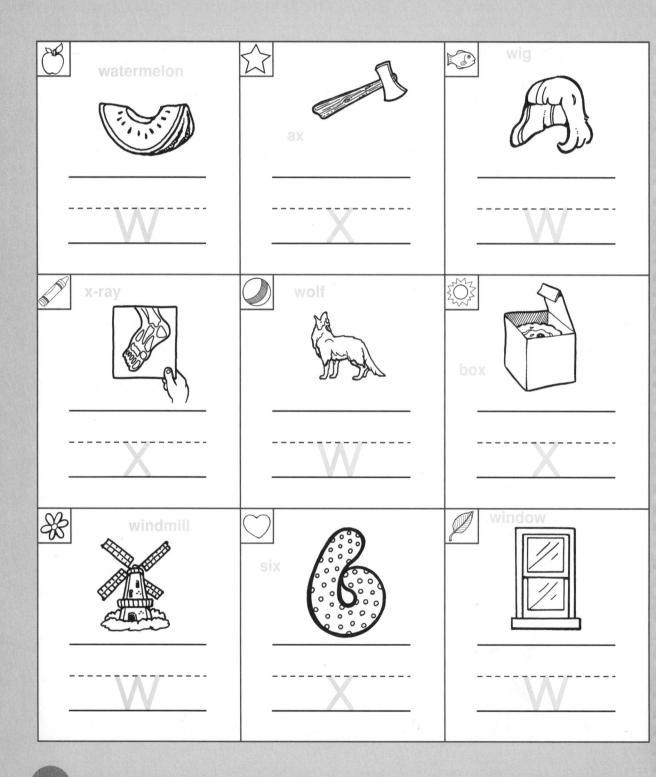

watermelon

ax

wig

x-ray

wolf

box

windmill

six

window

Name_____

Have children name and trace the letter Vv at the top of the page. Ask them to find and mark the letter Vv in the vans.

Name_____

V V V V   V V V

V V V V   V V V

Name_____

Vv

Have children name each picture and color the items whose names begin with the /v/ sound, as in *vulture*.

doll	van	pizza
valentine	turtle	vest
vase	vegetables	rainbow

Name_____

Ask children to listen for the beginning sound as you say the name of each picture. Have children write V or v on the lines if the picture name begins with the letter Vv.

vest

vegetables

elf

turkey

van

vase

vacuum

fish

volcano

Name_____

Jj

Have children name and trace the letter Jj at the top of the page. Ask them to find and mark the letter Jj in the jars.

Have children print Jj on the store roof. Then ask them to trace and write J and j on the lines.

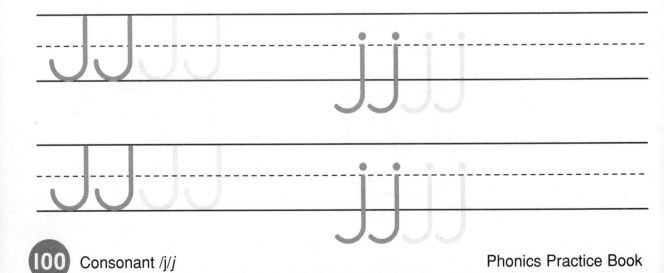

Name_____

Have children name each picture and color the items whose names begin with the /j/ sound, as in *jellyfish*.

jack-in-the-box

jet

van

lion

juice

axe

jeep

jump rope

ostrich

Name_____

Ask children to listen for the beginning sound as you say the name of each picture. Have children write J or j on the lines if the picture name begins with the letter Jj.

jump rope

egg

jacks

jeep

kangaroo

jar

juice

mushroom

jet

Phonics Practice Book

Name_____

Ee

Have children name and trace the letter Ee at the top of the page. Ask them to find and mark the letter Ee in the eggs.

Name

Scrambled eggs

Fried eggs

Boiled eggs

E E E E   e e e e

E E E E   e e e e

Name_____

Ee

Have children name each picture and color the items whose names begin with the /e/ sound, as in *elephant*.

egg

jack-in-the-box

guitar

envelope

elf

fox

koala

elevator

nuts

Phonics Practice Book

Vowel /e/e

Name _____

Ask children to listen for the beginning sound as you say the name of each picture. Have children write E or e on the lines if the picture name begins with the letter Ee.

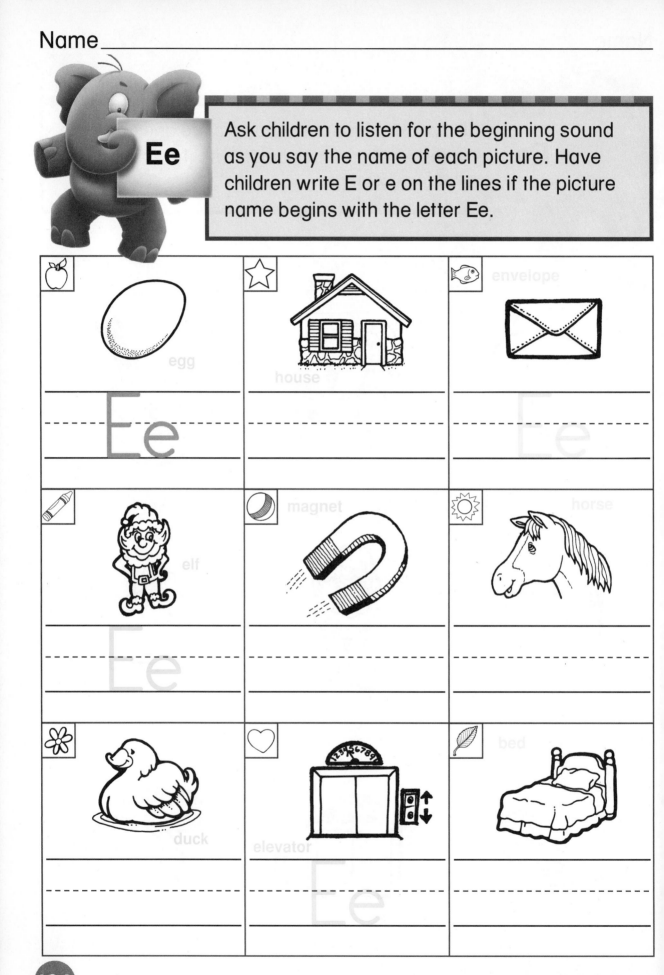

Name_____

Say the name of each picture. Then have children circle the letter that stands for its beginning sound.

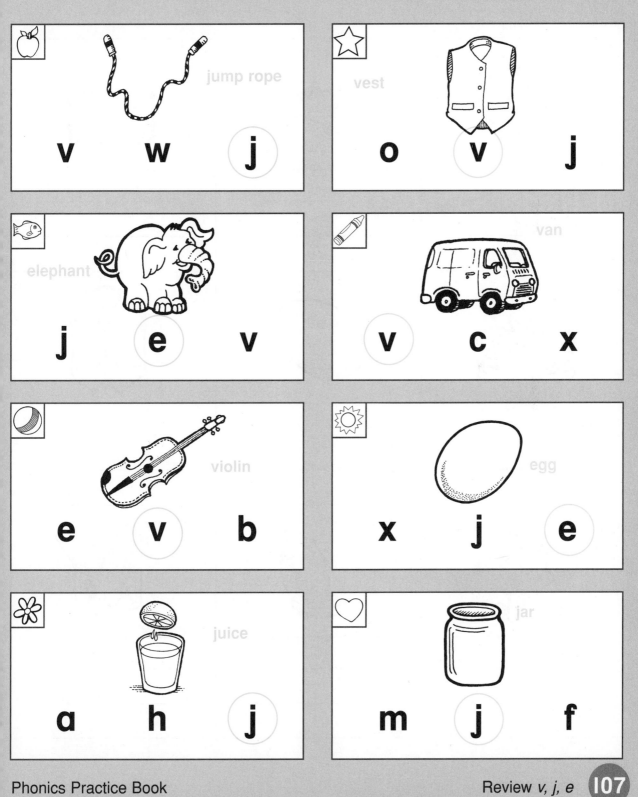

v   w   **j**

o   **v**   j

j   **e**   v

v   c   x

e   **v**   b

x   j   **e**

a   h   **j**

m   **j**   f

Name_____

Say the name of each picture. Then have children write the letter that stands for its beginning sound.

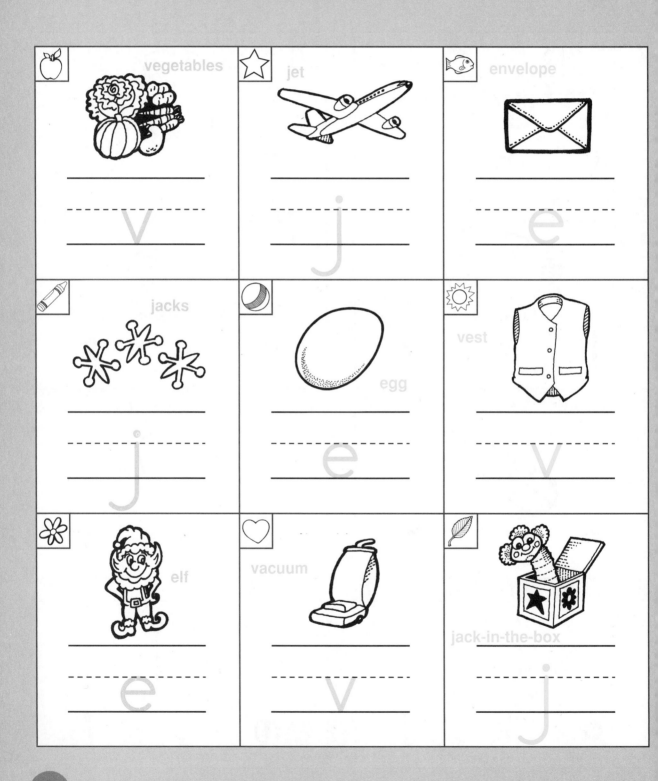

vegetables

v

jet

j

envelope

e

jacks

j

egg

e

vest

v

elf

e

vacuum

v

jack-in-the-box

j

Name_____

Yy

Have children name and trace the letter Yy at the top of the page. Ask them to find and mark the letter Yy in the yo-yos.

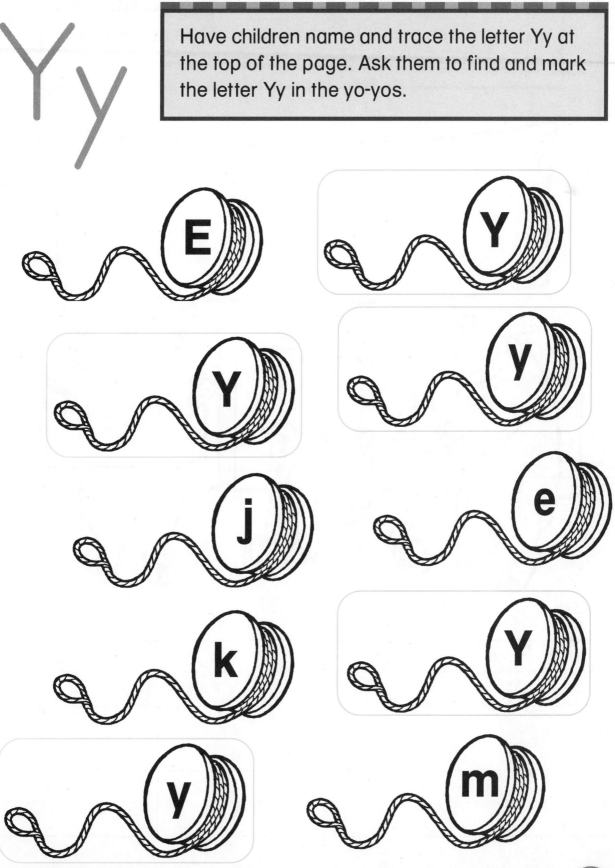

Name_____

Have children print Yy on the banner. Then ask them to trace and write Y and y on the lines.

Name_____

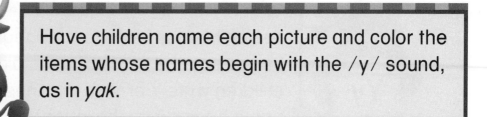

Have children name each picture and color the items whose names begin with the /y/ sound, as in *yak*.

yarn · apple · elephant

yolk · horse · yam

sink · jet · barn

Name _____

Ask children to listen for the beginning sound as you say the name of each picture. Have children write Y or y on the lines if the picture name begins with the letter Yy.

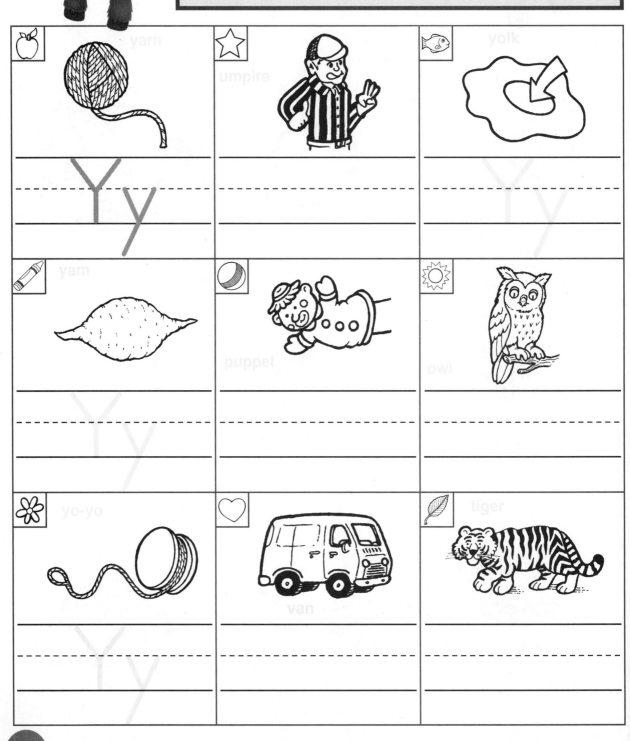

Name_____

Have children name and trace the letter Zz at the top of the page. Ask them to find and mark the letter Zz in the zebras.

Name_____

Have children print Zz on the zoo sign. Then ask them
to trace and write Z and z on the lines.

ZZZZ   zzzz

ZZZZ   zzzz

Name_____

Zz

Have children name each picture and color the items whose names begin with the /z/ sound, as in *zebra*.

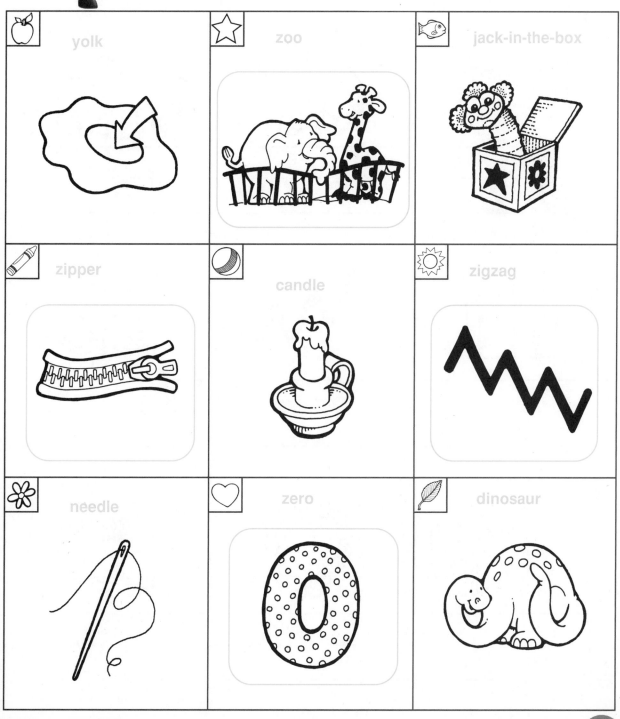

yolk	zoo	jack-in-the-box
zipper	candle	zigzag
needle	zero	dinosaur

Ask children to listen for the beginning sound as you say the name of each picture. Have children write Z or z on the lines if the picture name begins with the letter Zz.

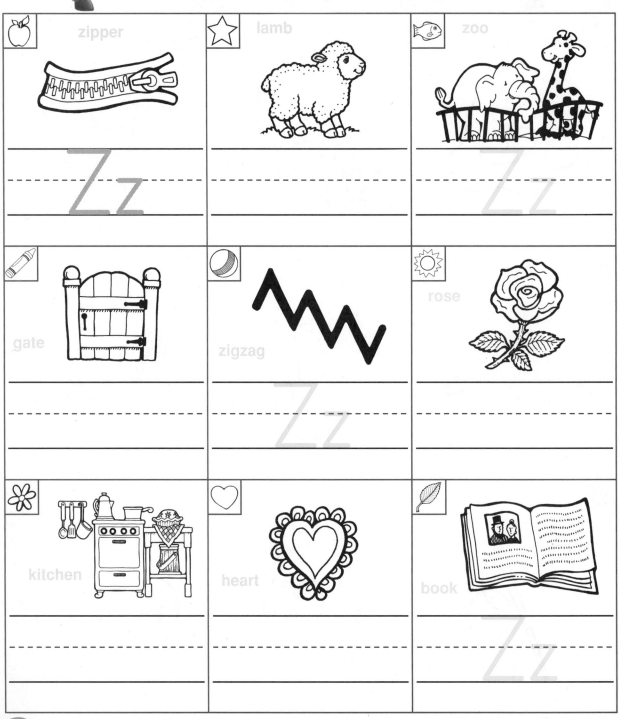

zipper

lamb

zoo

gate

zigzag

rose

kitchen

heart

book

Name_____

Say the name of each picture. Then have children circle the letter that stands for its beginning sound.

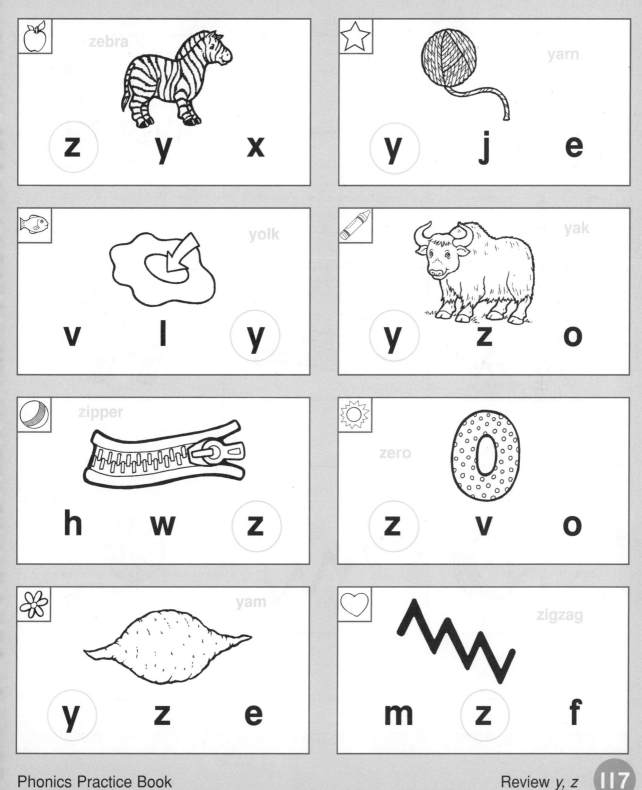

zebra
z   y   x

yarn
y   j   e

yolk
v   l   y

yak
y   z   o

zipper
h   w   z

zero
z   v   o

yam
y   z   e

zigzag
m   z   f

Name_____

Say the name of each picture. Then have children write the letter that stands for its beginning sound.

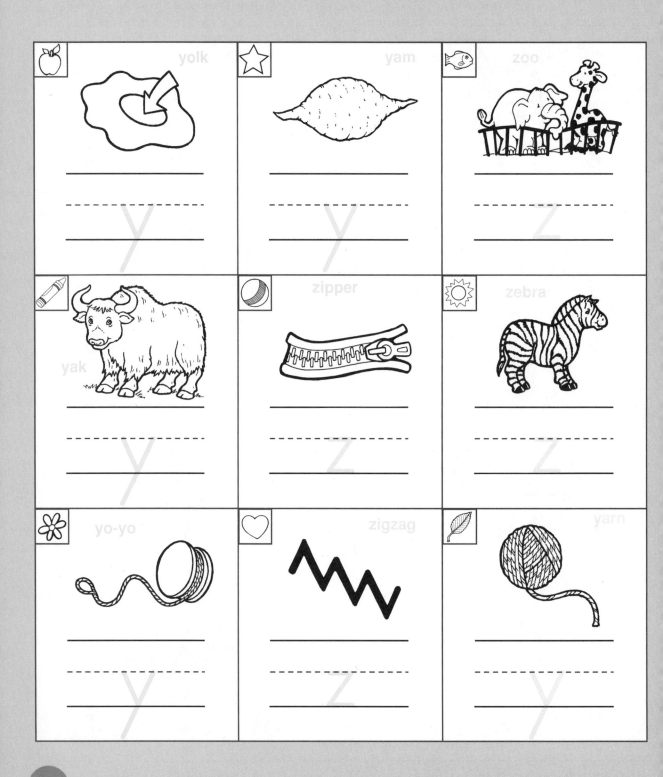

Name_____

Qq

Have children name and trace the letter Qq at the top of the page. Ask them to find and mark the letter Qq in the quilts.

Name_____

Have children print Qq above the queen. Then ask
them to trace and write Q and q on the lines.

Long Live
the
Queen!

QQQQ qqqq

QQQQ qqqq

Name_____

Have children name each picture and color the items whose names begin with the /kw/ sound, as in *quail*.

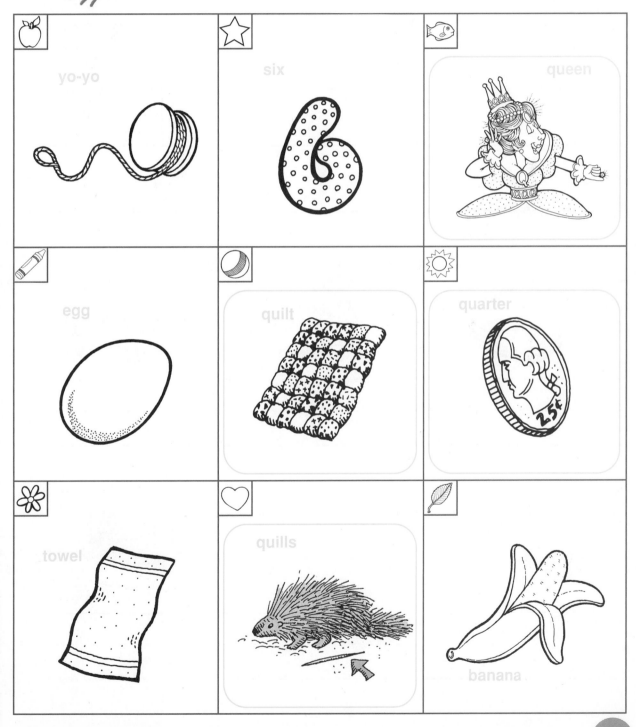

yo-yo

six

queen

egg

quilt

quarter

towel

quills

banana

Consonant /kw/q

Qq

Ask children to listen for the beginning sound as you say the name of each picture. Have children write Q or q on the lines if the picture name begins with the letter Qq.

quarter	hand	nurse
Qq		

sandwich	queen	jeep
	Qq	

quilt	ostrich	quills
Qq		Qq

Name

Uu

Have children name and trace the letter Uu at the top of the page. Ask them to find and mark the letter Uu in the umbrellas.

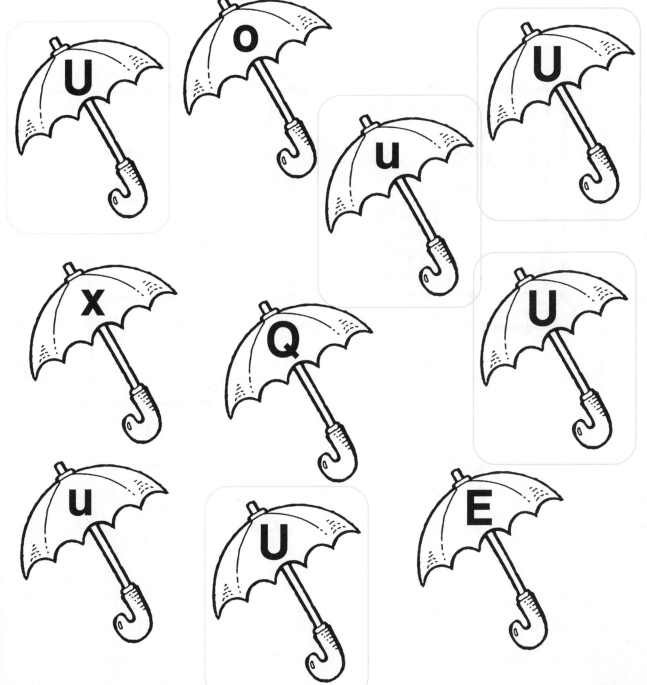

Name_____

Umbrellas for Sale

Phonics Practice Book

Name _____

Uu

Have children name each picture and color the items whose names begin with the /u/ sound, as in *umbrella*.

under	lamp	cake
belt	umpire	seal
turkey	juice	up

Name_____

Uu

Ask children to listen for the beginning sound as you say the name of each picture. Have children write U or u on the lines if the picture name begins with the letter Uu.

umpire	jar	necklace
Uu		

under	yo-yo	car
Uu		

mouse	up	towel
	Uu	

Vowel /u/u

Name_____

Say the name of each picture. Then have children circle the letter that stands for its beginning sound.

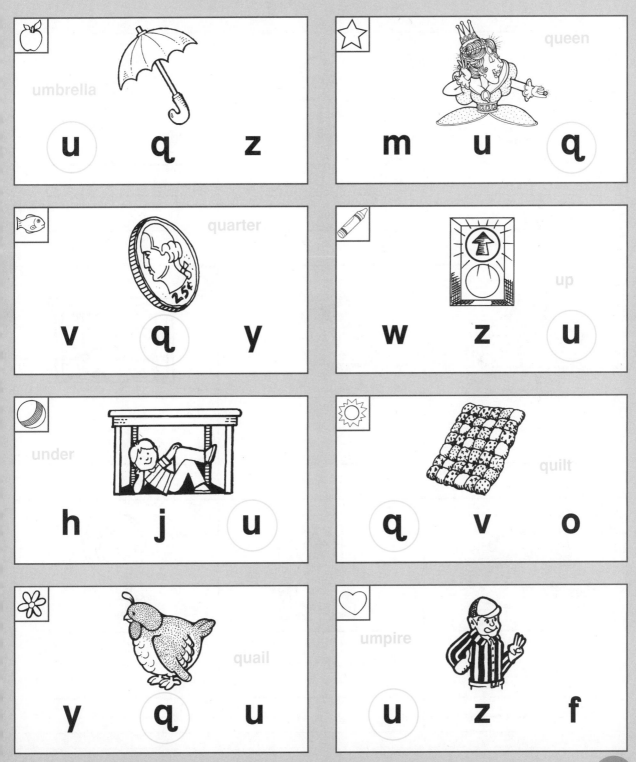

u   q   z

m   u   q

v   q   y

w   z   u

h   j   u

q   v   o

y   q   u

u   z   f

Name _____

REVIEW

Say the name of each picture. Then have children write the letter that stands for its beginning sound.

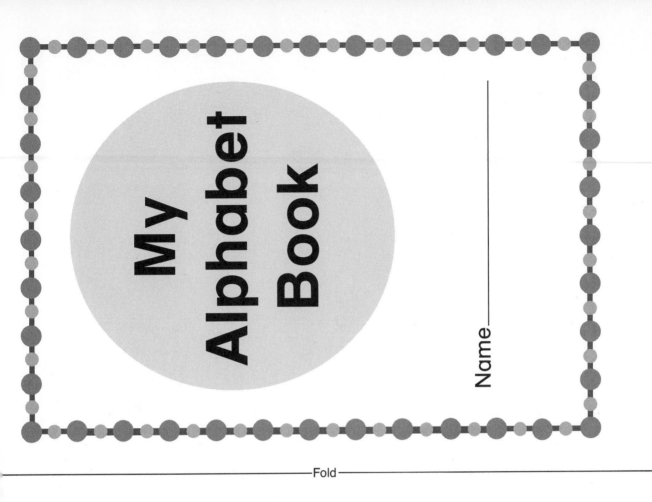

My
Alphabet
Book

Name _____

-Fold-

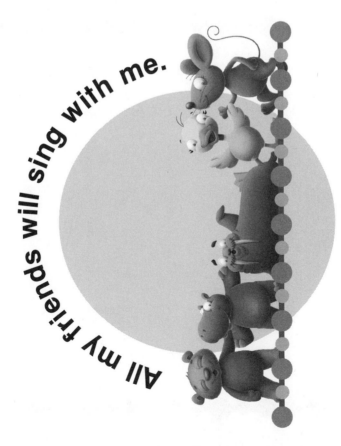

All my friends will sing with me.

Directions: Help your child cut out and fold up the book.

Cut-out/Fold-up Book

Fold

Date

I Can Say My ABC's!

(Draw a self portrait.)

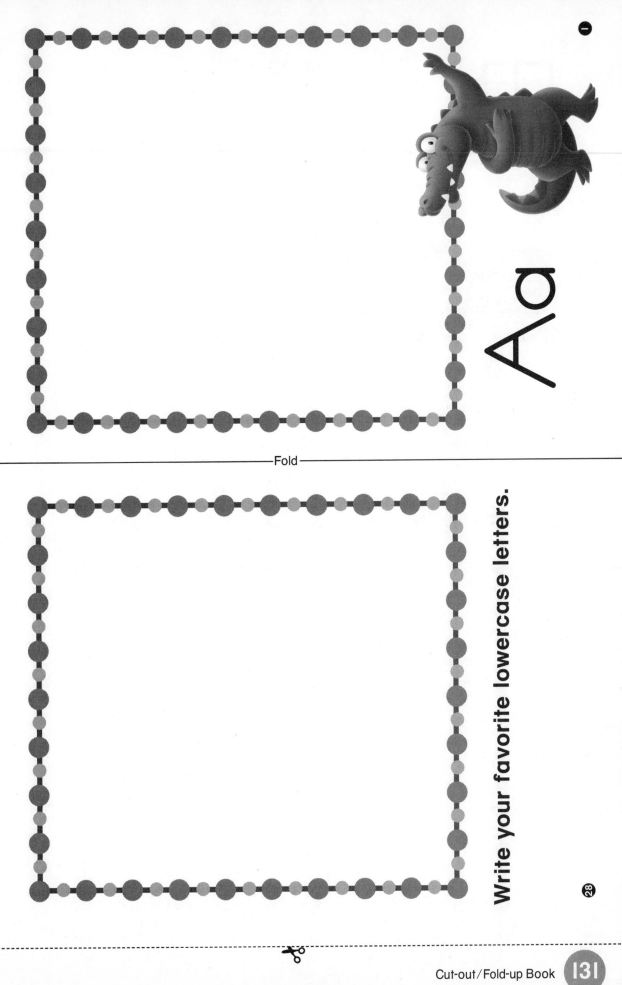

Fold

Aa

Write your favorite lowercase letters.

28

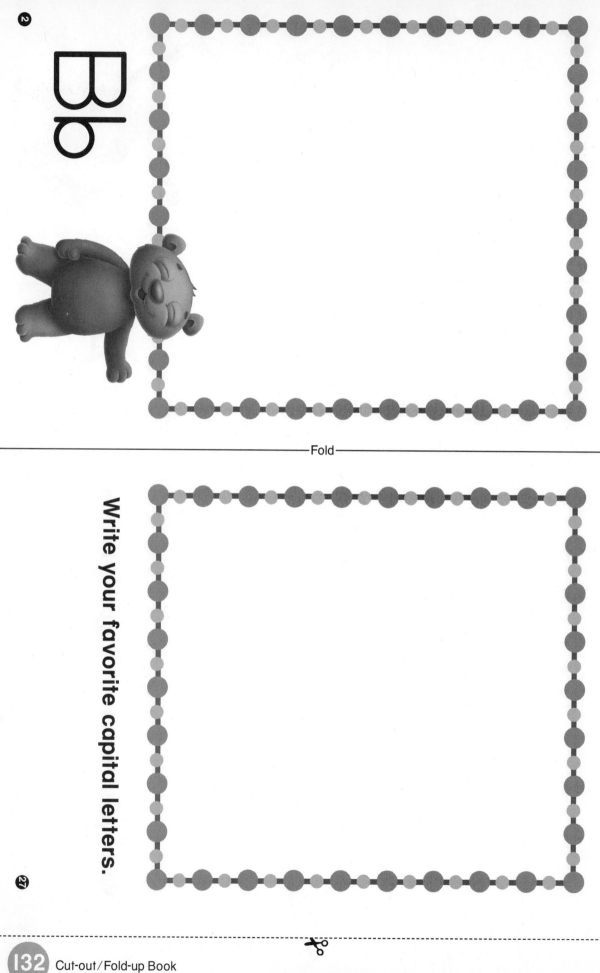

Bb

Fold

Write your favorite capital letters.

2

27

Cc

③

Fold

Zz

㉖

✂

Cut-out / Fold-up Book 133

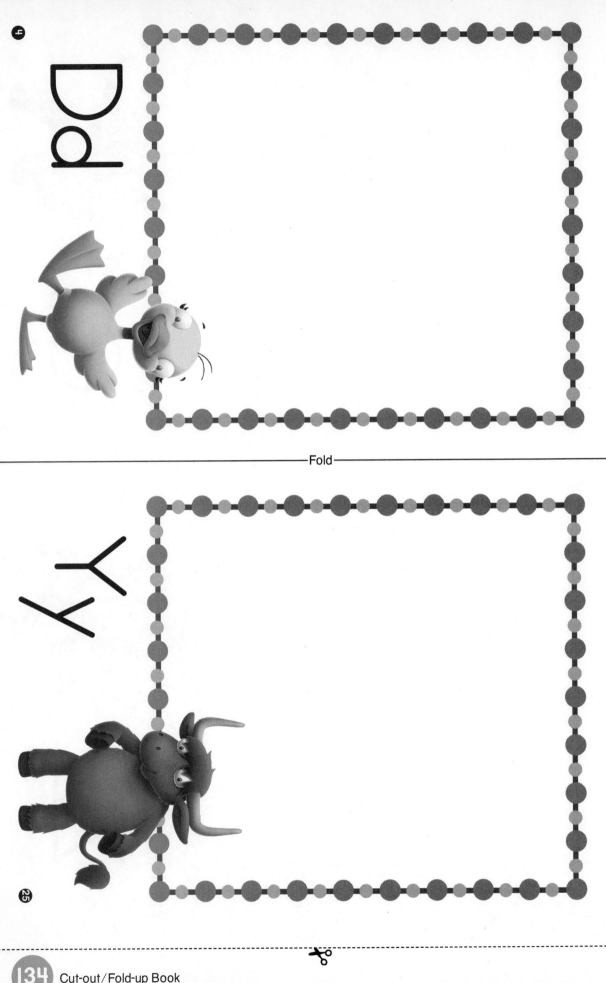

4

Dd

Fold

Yy

25

Cut-out/Fold-up Book

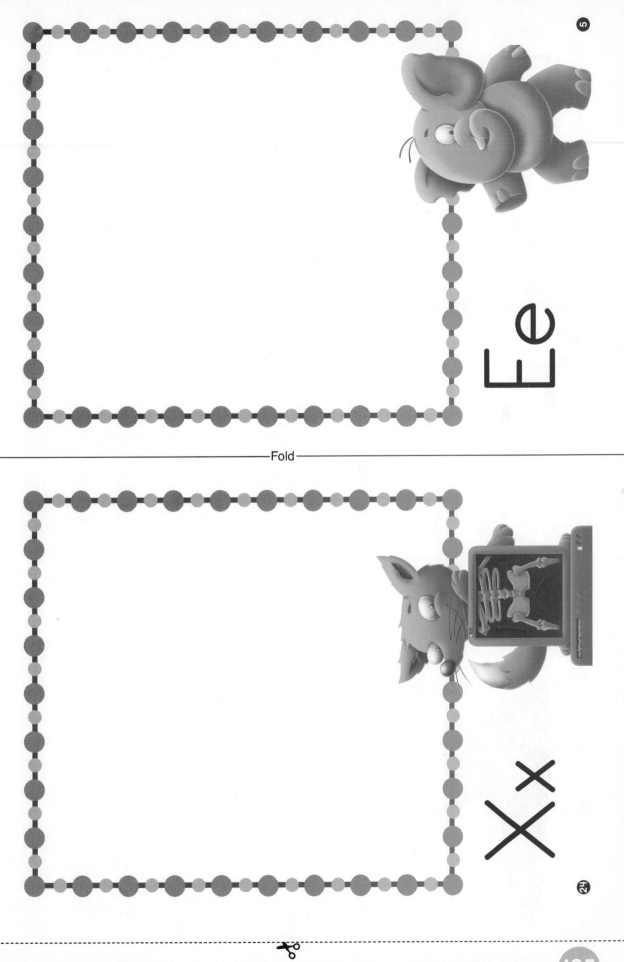

Ee

Fold

Xx

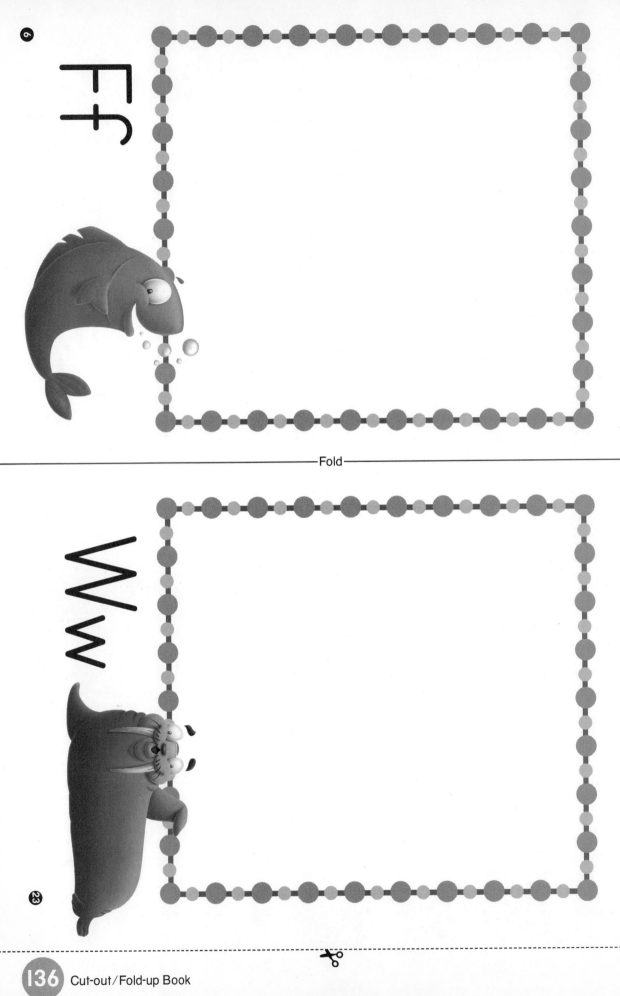

Ff

6

Fold

Ww

23

Cut-out/Fold-up Book

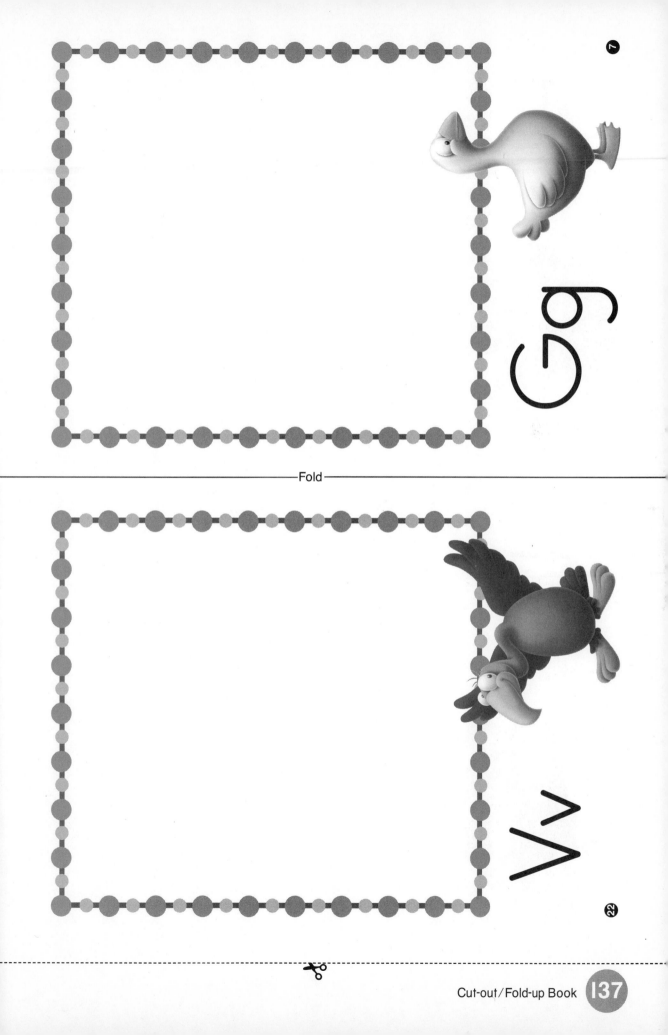

Gg

Fold

Vv

✂

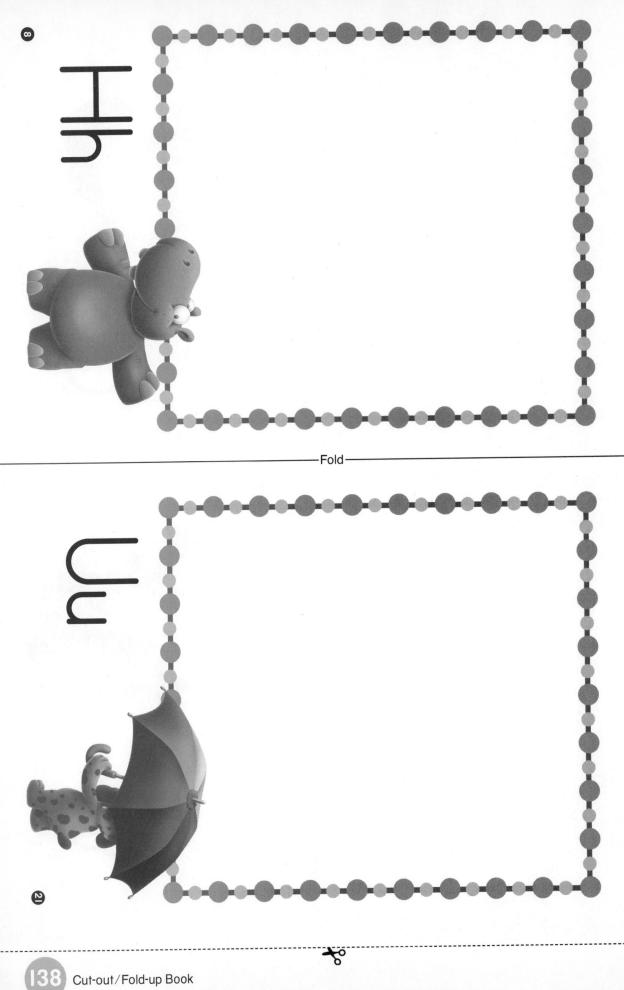

8

Hh

Fold

Uu

21

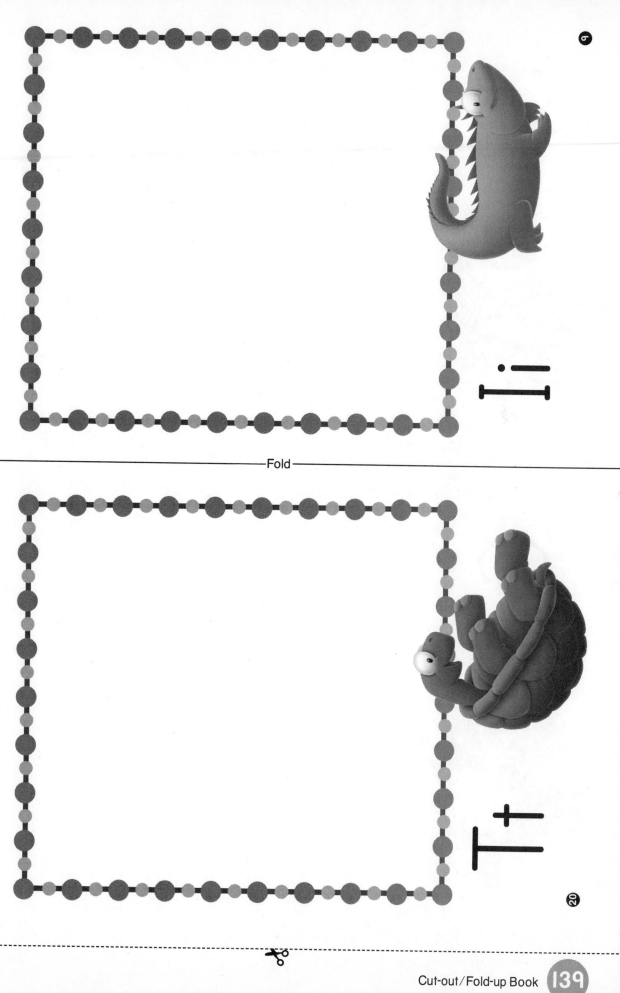

Ii

Tt

9

20

Fold

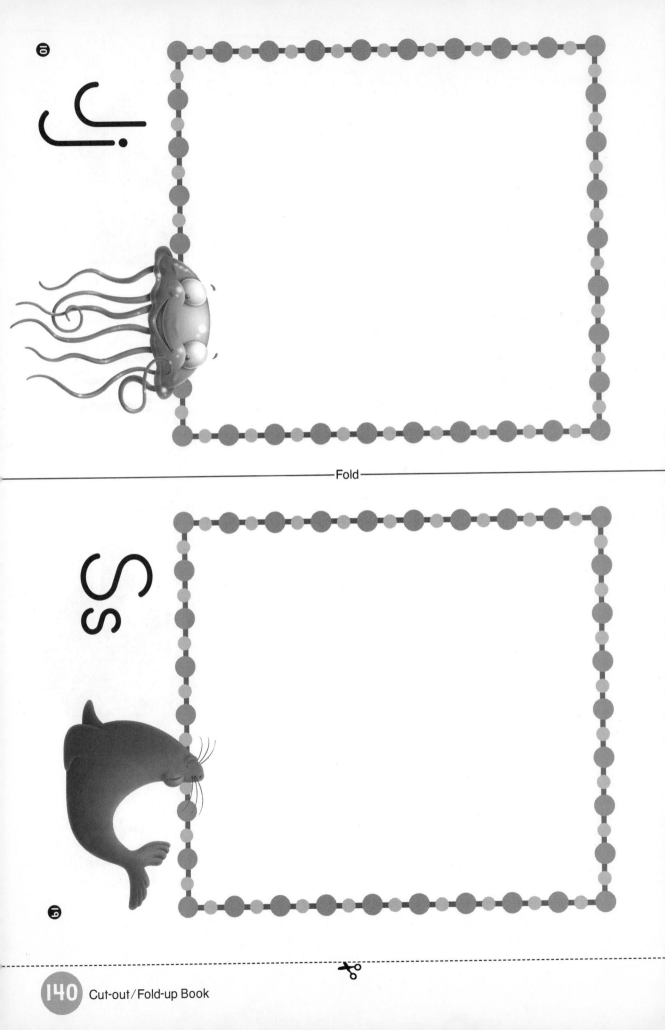

Jj

Ss

Fold

Kk

— Fold —

Rr

Ll

12

Fold

Qq

17

Cut-out/Fold-up Book

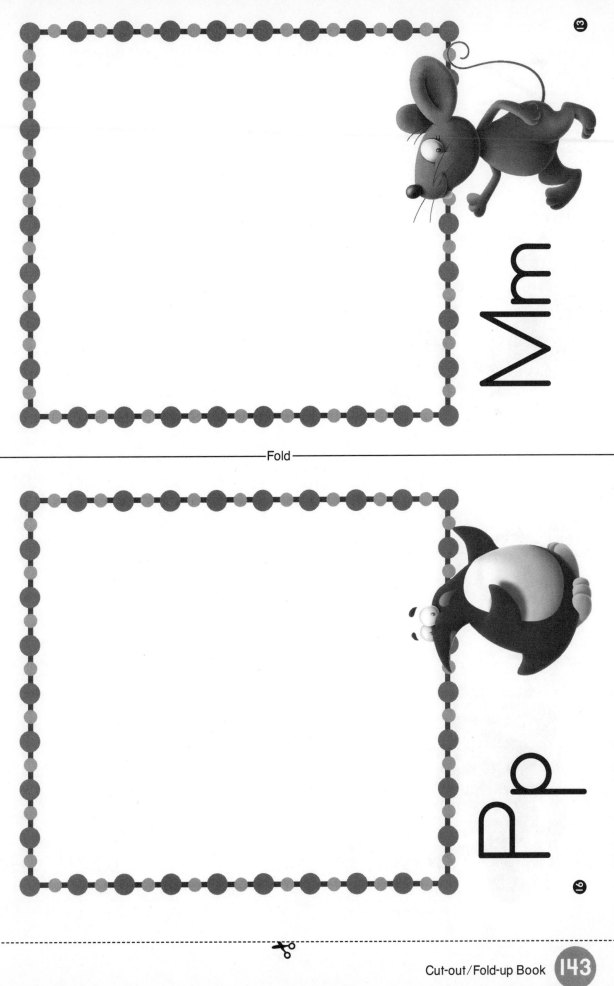

Mm

(13)

—Fold—

Pp

(16)

Cut-out/Fold-up Book **143**

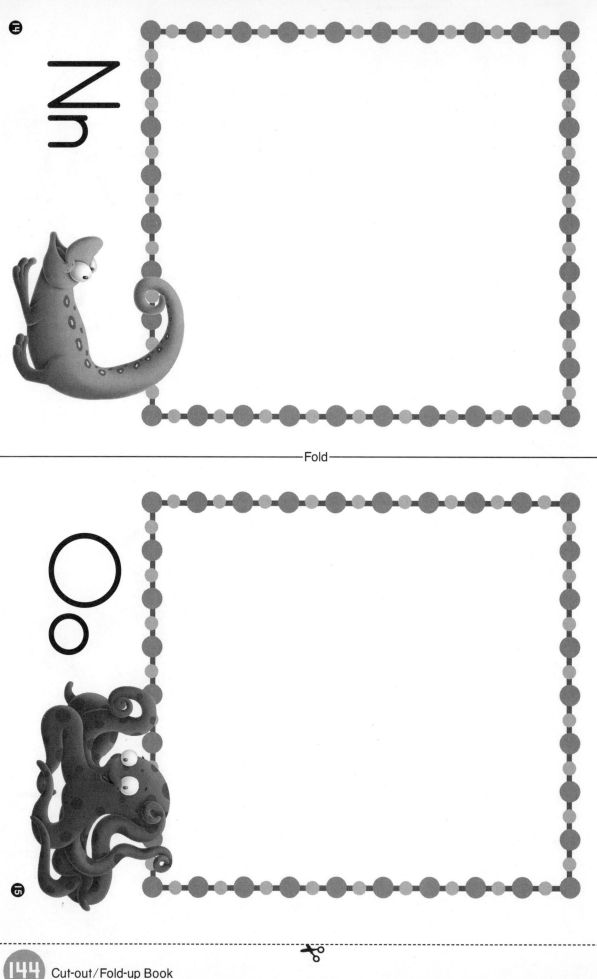

14

Nn

Fold

Oo

15

Cut-out/Fold-up Book